DAISY, DAISY

Christian Miller

DAISY, DAISY

A Journey Across America on a Bicycle

DOUBLEDAY & COMPANY, INC.
GARDEN CITY, NEW YORK
1981

Library of Congress Cataloging in Publication Data
Miller, Christian.
Daisy, Daisy.
1. Bicycle touring—United States.   2. United States—
Description and travel—1960
I. Title.
GV1045.M54   1981   917.3
ISBN: 0-385-17475-6
Library of Congress Catalog Card Number 80-2946

For Carl Heckstall, my eldest grandson,
who can bicycle much faster

CONTENTS

CONTENTS

DAISY, DAISY

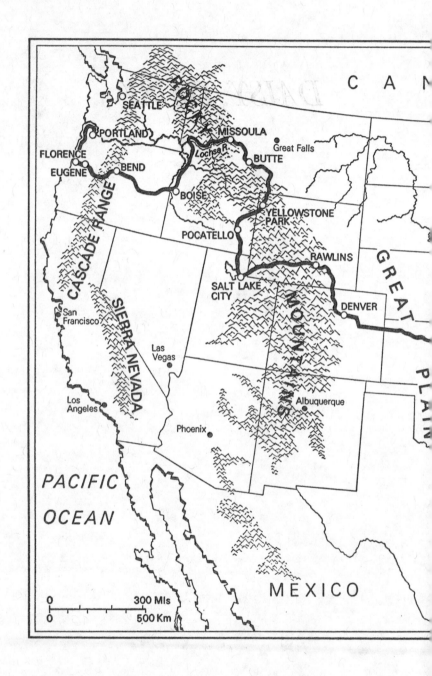

CANADA

Minneapolis

Detroit

Chicago

Pittsburgh

Boston

New York

Philadelphia

Indianapolis

Cincinnati

Washington

KANSAS
CITY

ST LOUIS

LOUISVILLE

RICHMOND

LENE

LEXINGTON

YORKTOWN

chita

Nashville

ahoma City

Memphis

Atlanta

allas

ATLANTIC
OCEAN

APPALACHIAN   MOUNTAINS

Mississippi River

New Orleans

GULF OF MEXICO

Miami

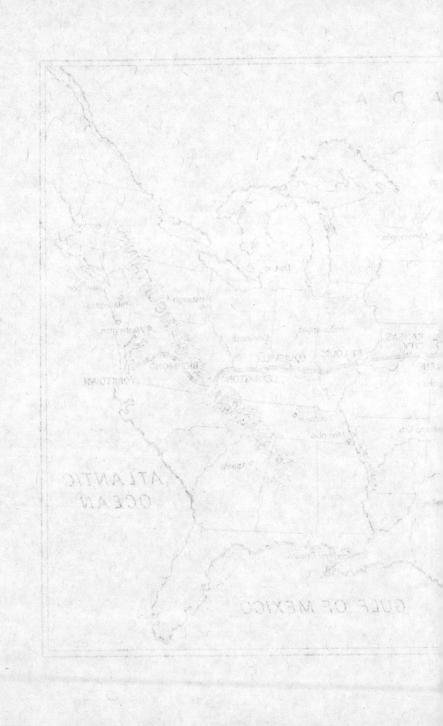

GETTING AWAY

"Are you really quite sure this is what you want?" said the travel agent.

His fingers—distributed among the pages of his American brochure—were spread out like those of a woman waiting for her nail-varnish to dry. One was inserted at the page marked "Pacific Coast—14 days with escort," the next at "New York—taste the Big Apple," the third at a page headed "Disneyland—the ultimate in family holidays," while his smallest finger had vanished completely behind a head-on photograph of a Greyhound bus. Clearly, he was determined to keep all options open.

I paused in the middle of writing out a cheque.

"You mean, am I quite sure I want a ticket to the east coast of America, and another back from the west? Yes."

"But madam—forgive my asking—how exactly are you planning to cross the States? If you would like us to make bookings for you on domestic flights, inside the States. . . ."

"No, really," I said—quite mildly, considering I didn't feel under any obligation to tell him—"I'm planning to bicycle."

The travel agent caught the eye of his assistant who, behind a propped-up copy of *The Holidaymaker's Guide to the Canaries*, was surreptitiously leafing through a fashion magazine; she shrugged a dismissive shoulder, signalling that she had no intention of getting involved. Then he looked out of the window at the afternoon bustle of our country town, as if willing one of the shoppers to come in, shed her winter anorak, and book a standard holiday in Torremolinos. Finally, with a disapproving sigh, he resigned himself to writing out my ticket, which read London-Washington, Portland-London.

Washington (DC) was, according to my maps, fairly near the Atlantic, and Portland (Oregon) close to the Pacific, and nothing that the travel agent said was going to put me off my plan, which was to bicycle across America from one ocean to the other. I was determined partly because I really wanted to get to know America, and partly because bicycling, with all its uncertainties, would give me a good excuse for not saying exactly where I was going to be.

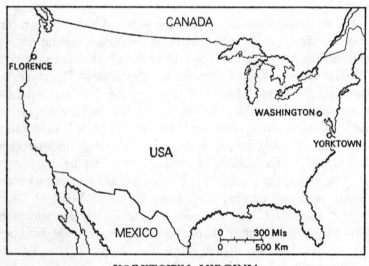

YORKTOWN, VIRGINIA

All my life I had had to let other people know where I could be found. When I was a young girl my mother had insisted on knowing who I was with and what I was planning to do; after I married and had children I hadn't even been able to go out to dinner without naming the restaurant; when the children grew older I had left telephone numbers at their schools, so that I could be reached in an emergency, and as my mother became progressively more frail I found myself back where I had started —never leaving home without letting her, or one of my sisters, know where I could be found.

This all seemed perfectly natural at the time, but then one morning I woke up and realised—with considerable amazement —that nobody needed, any more, to know where I was. My mother had died, my children had grown up and my grand-children belonged to them, not to me; my husband was happily occupied, and I myself had no job to tie me down. I was, at last, completely my own master, and if I didn't take advantage of this freedom I would have only myself to blame. So I thought I would take myself off on a little trip; I would go completely alone, and for the very first time in my life I wouldn't leave addresses behind.

Once I had bought the ticket, the only thing left to do was to collect the necessary gear.

Obviously, I needed a bicycle. Apart from the children's, the only one in the family was a sit-up-and-beg veteran that I occa-sionally used to run down to the post office; the post office was about a hundred yards from our drive gate and the trip was the longest I normally felt inclined to tackle—anything further and I got out the car. It was a stalwart old bicycle, but as airlines won't carry a normal machine unless it's crated I decided to get a new, folding one, and being incapable of understanding tech-nical jargon about gear ratios, front sprockets and so on, I sim-ply picked the smallest and lightest one on the market; it was alloy and stainless steel, with a very small back wheel and an even smaller front one.

"What are you going to call it?" asked my eldest grandson, surveying it a bit doubtfully.

"I wasn't planning to call it anything, really."

"You should."

I thought hard.

"I know!" I said. "How about that song, 'Daisy, Daisy'?"

"Was that about a bicycle?"

"A tandem—a bicycle made for two."

"Well, how about just 'Daisy,' then? A bicycle made for one, sort-of?"

So the bicycle was christened Daisy. The next thing to find was a light-weight tent; I wanted to keep within the airline 22-kilo free baggage allowance, and as Daisy weighed 11, this only left me with another 11 for everything else. Eventually I found a Scandinavian tent that was not only amazingly light but was also a nice smudgy colour, which meant that with any luck I would be able to put it up even in places where tourists tents were usually forbidden, such as the front lawn of the White House. My extra-light-weight mountaineering sleeping-bag, on the other hand, looked like a conspicuously moribund circus clown, being bright blue and orange with a little (empty) pointy hood at the top.

"That's to pull over your head when the temperature goes down below freezing," the sales assistant explained helpfully.

"Oh," I answered confidently. "I won't need that—I'll never sleep out in cold weather." Little did I know.

The tent and sleeping-bag weighed, together, about 4 kilos, so I was now down to roughly 7 kilos for all the other essentials of rugged travel. I put up a paper-hanger's table in my bedroom, and set out all the things I thought I would need. And then I weighed everything. Clearly, I wasn't going to get it all on a bicycle—I'd have to hire a van.

Night after night, I lay in bed studying the things on that table, and every morning I took something off. I asked myself "Is it possible to live without it?" and if it was, off it went. Eventually I got down to a basic survival kit of tent, sleeping-bag and rudimentary cooking gear, essential documents such as my passport, traveller's cheques and maps, a book called *Geography of the United States*, a repair outfit for Daisy, some washing things, and a travel-size bottle of Diorissimo.

Clothes? You could almost say I didn't pack any, because I stood up in most of them—jeans, an anorak, some canvas shoes, a sweater. Underclothes? I took none at all, because everything that I planned to wear under my other clothes in cold weather could also be used as top-clothes when the temperature rose—instead of a bra and pants, for instance, I decided to take a bikini, and as an extra layer for really cold conditions I slipped in a boy's navy cotton vest that I would also be able to use as a sleeveless "top" in a heatwave.

Just about my only concession to respectability was a two-piece cotton voile dress; it squashed up to almost nothing and the top part could be used over my jeans, while the skirt half could go under either my sweater or the navy vest.

Everything in this positively Parisian wardrobe was either navy blue or fawn, the former because it would tie in with the one basic item—the navy blue jeans—and the latter because it wouldn't show the dust.

My family were all very nice about my plans to go away, taking the view that if I wanted to go I might as well *go*, rather than just spend the next few years sitting around wishing that I had. Indeed, everyone was so nonchalant about my leaving that when the day of departure actually arrived I suddenly became convinced that nobody would miss me at all, and practically had to be dragged to the airport. It was, incidentally, April 1st—All Fools' Day—but everyone tactfully avoided rubbing this in.

Now Daisy, when folded, packed into a smallish canvas bag, and because she was, when collapsed like this, easily damaged, I'd been allowed to carry her on to the plane as hand-baggage. It was the height of the hijacking scare, and already, when leaving Heathrow, I had had to unpack her, to show that she wasn't some sort of weapon, and when I arrived at Washington airport, the monitor screen of the X-ray scanner again flickered a warning.

"Step this way, please," said the security guard. "Perhaps you'd care to tell me what you are carrying?"

"Of course. A bicycle."

"A bicycle?" He looked at the bag with an air of weary disbelief. "Unpack, please."

I didn't like getting Daisy in and out of her bag, which was, if

anything, a shade too small for her, and on top of that, I'd secured the bag with several bits of rope, tied with lumpy amateur
knots. Obviously, though, this was no time to argue, so I picked
the knots undone, got her out, set her up, broke her down again,
forced her back into her bag, and re-did all the knots.

Just down the line a customs official was waiting for me.

"Unpack, please."

"But I've just . . ."

He looked at me impassively. "Unpack, please."

I undid the knots again, but before I'd had time to get Daisy
out the customs man had thrust his hand into the bag. Outraged,
Daisy struck at him with a pedal.

"Goddammit!" he howled, retreating into a back room, osten-
sibly to get disinfectant put on his wound but, I suspected, also
to look up some way of charging import duty on dangerous bicycles. Trying to show a willingness to co-operate, I again wrestled
Daisy out of her bag and set her up. The man came back, osten-
tatiously holding up a bandaged finger.

"What's that . . . that bit of machinery doing here?"

"I thought you wanted me to unpack . . . ?"

"Just move along, please. Move along. Next, please."

Normally I managed to fit all my main stuff into a rucksack,
while my money and passport went into a small canvas shoulder-
bag. This meant that when Daisy was folded, I carried her in
one hand, slung my rucksack and the canvas bag over my shoulders, and still had the other hand free to deal with such things
as boarding cards. But this was no moment to loiter over loading
up; I hustled Daisy to the door, dragging the rest of my gear
after me.

Outside the airport building I got myself ready for the road.
The rucksack went on Daisy's back carrier, snapped—by means
of two of those fasteners that come on the ends of dog-leads—to
the springs on the underside of the seat. A stretchy cord, of the
kind one uses to stop luggage blowing off a car roof-rack, went
round the middle of the rucksack and secured it to Daisy's seat
tube (the vertical bit of tubing that a bike's seat rests on). As it

was a pretty fat rucksack it must have looked, when seen from behind, rather like a podgy baby wearing a tight belt, but the arrangement was surprisingly secure, and although—as you'll hear later—disaster might overtake my entire bundle of tricks, I never suffered the indignity of shedding my gear on the road.

More short stretchy cords fixed my tent's aluminium poles to the front of the seat tube, and Daisy's own travelling bag, now that she was out of it, hung over her own handlebars, making it a very convenient receptacle for my shoulder-bag, maps, and any other odds and ends that I might need when actually on the road.

Feeling a little dazed—for the clocks were trying to tell me that it was morning while my body was insisting that it was nearly bedtime—I wobbled off down my first American road.

Apart from a brief circular spin round my own yard, I had never ridden Daisy before. I had nursed a secret fear that if I tried some practice runs on her I might find I didn't like bicycling, and I had felt the same way about doing any physical training—I had been quite sure that if I had so much as taken even the tiniest bit of extra exercise to prepare me for the ride, I would have found that some bit of me ached so badly that I would have been put off the whole idea. So when I set out that first morning, I was on an unknown bicycle, and my muscles weren't only unknown—they and I had barely been introduced.

I had managed to start in the morning rush-hour. Vast American cars hurtled at me from all sides, honking their horns and drenching me with spray, for it had also started to pour with rain. I hadn't tightened the fasteners of the collapsible handlebars tightly enough, and the handlebars were moving jerkily in almost every direction except the one in which I was trying to steer. My heels kept hitting the sides of the rucksack on the back carrier and my anorak seemed to be rapidly turning into a sieve. Within ten minutes I was soaked to the skin, the brim of my denim hat clinging to my forehead like a licked postage-stamp.

To add to my joys I was having to bicycle—for the first time in my life—on the right-hand side of the road; this wasn't all that bad on the straight stretches but when it came to roundabouts it was about as easy as trying to make bath-water spin the wrong way down a plug-hole.

I had been determined to start my journey actually on the shore of the Atlantic; the airport had been some miles inland, so I was, for the moment, heading back towards England, and when the ocean came into view I remember thinking that even if I had swum it I couldn't have been wetter. All of a sudden, at the edge of the parkway along which I was travelling, I spotted a big museum, with a sign proclaiming that it boasted a Coffee Shop. Thankfully, I chained Daisy to some railings and went in.

I was half-way through a bowl of tomato soup when I noticed a man advancing on me brandishing a stick. As I had by now realised that the entire museum was dedicated to the culmination of the American War of Independence I thought for one scary moment that he might be a particularly loyal citizen who'd spotted that one of the perfidious oppressors was trying to get back in. But then I saw that there was a mop on the end of the stick.

"Excuse me, ma'am, but would you care to raise your feet?"

I looked down. Around the legs of my chair a large puddle was forming, increasing even as I looked by more and more water dripping into it from my clothes. The man followed me morosely round the museum, mopping up the little pools that formed whenever I paused to look at paintings of shivering British troops declining to charge at blazing American cannon. Being so obviously a member of the Baddy side was too much for me; I fled to the sea-shore and gazed in a homesick way in the direction of England—3,000 miles away over grey and stormy waves. Then I went into what seemed to be the only sea-front hotel.

"May I have a room for one night, please? And could I leave my bicycle somewhere under cover?"

As it was so early in the season, and there had only been a couple of cars standing outside, I felt certain that the hotel wouldn't be full. But the man behind the desk seemed doubtful. "I'll just check. I'm not sure if we have a vacancy."

He vanished behind one of those walls made of strips of looking-glass; I couldn't see through it, but I knew very well that he could look in the opposite direction—outwards—and I sensed that both he and the person with whom he was having a whispered conversation were studying me apprehensively.

"I'm so sorry," he said, coming back and supporting himself on the counter on the tips of his outspread fingers. "But it seems that we're fully booked tonight. Perhaps if you went to the airport . . . ?"

"But I've just come from the airport," I wailed. "And I'm absolutely exhausted. Haven't you got *anything*?"

But he and whoever lurked behind the mirrors had clearly just formulated a new house rule—No Wet Women on Bicycles. As I made for the door, I left frog-like footmarks on their classy carpet. I stood outside the hotel, wondering what to do; I couldn't see any other building that looked like a hotel and the idea of putting up my tent was not only depressing but would, I felt sure, lead to a nasty case of pneumonia.

Suddenly the door of the hotel swung open behind me and an elegant little golden-haired figure stepped briskly out.

"What nonsense," she announced. "Just because they had some trouble with hippy bicyclists last summer. I've given them what-for, I can tell you."

She jerked an umbrella open and thrust it forcefully upwards, as if to demonstrate the sort of what-for she'd been handing out. "Now, how about coming to stay with me, at my house?"

Daisy fitted easily into the enormous boot of her car. We swept at break-neck speed through the narrow streets of the little town and pulled up with jaw-snapping suddenness outside a neat one-storey house. It was made of wood, like almost all the houses I was going to see in America; the plants in the greenhouse attached to one end seemed to be pressing their faces to the glass, like children watching at a window to see who is coming up the drive. I felt instantly at home.

In a borrowed dressing-gown, I sat in the cosy living-room,

sipping a reviving drink. My clothes were steaming over a hot-water cylinder and from the kitchen came the appetising smell of roasting chicken. It was my first experience of the amazing hospitality that Americans show to strangers, and it filled me with a glow that was far from being only physical.

The next day the rain had completely vanished, and the sun was shining like it must have done on the day the Ark grounded. I crossed the centre of Yorktown, where the earthworks thrown up by the English general Lord Cornwallis (who, in 1781, made a last unsuccessful stand in Yorktown against the soldiers of the American Revolution) still ridged the pleasant parkland. The very first Purple Heart had been won by an American sergeant, storming those earthworks. George Washington had established it as a badge of military merit, but only three were awarded before the original purple cloth version fell into disuse, to be revived in the 1930s as a medal with a white-edged purple ribbon. I bicycled around for a bit, admiring the eighteenth-century cannons that decorated the earthworks; then I turned my back on the Atlantic and headed down the first mile of the westward trip.

The question of how many more miles lay ahead was just a little embarrassing. When I had first calculated the possible length of my journey the answer had come out as 2,400 miles, but then my husband had grabbed a pencil and pointed out that I had got the figures reversed—it was more like 4,200.

But as even 2,400 miles had seemed quite impossible for me to bicycle, the fact that it might be 4,200 didn't much worry me. It was a bit like trying to think of light years; who really bothers if a star is 10 or 10,000 light years away? Both figures are quite beyond an ordinary mortal's comprehension. And it was like that, for me, about the size of America—however big or little it was, the only thing that really concerned me was that I was going to start pedalling on one side of it, and go on pedalling till I got to the other side. The distance in between was of academic interest only, and when my milometer fell off just outside Yorktown I was really rather relieved—from then on, I wouldn't have to struggle to keep to a set daily mileage. I could just keep on going and see what happened.

The very first thing that happened was that I got ravenously hungry. I hadn't yet learnt the first golden rule for bicyclists, which is Even if You're Travelling through Jamaica, Always Carry a Few Bananas. I was bicycling down a beautiful parkway, lined with dogwood trees in the full glory of their spring blossom, and I was so dreadfully hungry that the branches took on a hallucinatory air of tables spread with white bread sandwiches. I was far too hungry even to turn off the road to look at James- town, the now almost-deserted spot where King James's first English colonists landed in 1607. But suddenly I found myself outside what must surely have been one of the world's biggest restaurants.

I couldn't believe my eyes—one minute I'd been on a virtually empty road, and the next I was in the middle of a crowd of peo- ple and was gazing—entranced—at an apparently endless counter piled with food. I grabbed a tray and got into line. Steak, fried potatoes, salad, apple pie, cheese, coffee—I piled the tray so high that I could barely stagger with it to a table. "Where am I?" I asked the man sitting opposite me. He looked mildly surprised. "Williamsburg," he said.

Now, although I'd done a lot of work on maps before I left home, and knew roughly where I was going, I still—not having been taught American history at school—had only a random smattering of knowledge about the places. For instance, I knew that when George Washington, the first president, was only twenty-seven, he'd owned 15,000 acres of land round Williams- burg—a little parcel that would have been worth, nowadays, enough to keep the entire continent supplied with cherry trees. I also knew that in 1716 the very first American theatre had been built in Williamsburg, for, as the sponsors put it, "the acting of comedies and drolls," and that in 1752, 136 years after Shake- speare's death, the first English company had arrived to put on a performance of *The Merchant of Venice*. What I didn't know was that a whole district of Williamsburg had been re-built with reproductions of the houses that used to stand there in Washington's time, and that the place had become one of the great tourist attractions of America.

I bicycled happily around (cars were not allowed in the rebuilt district), and admired the pretty wooden houses, rather wishing that someone hadn't told me that the "real" Williamsburg could never have looked like the re-built version, because it would have been impossible for all the houses—many of them of different periods—to have been in such mint condition at the same time. When my legs finally gave out I ate another vast meal and, finding myself a bed in what appeared to be a cheap hotel, fell into an exhausted sleep.

I hadn't paid much attention to the fact that my room had four beds in it—I'd just thought it was some sort of family room, for people travelling with children—so when the door burst open in what seemed to me to be the middle of the night I felt distinctly aggrieved. I groped for the light; it revealed three strapping people, dragging what seemed to be orange elephants through the door.

"Go away," I mumbled. "This is my room."

"Number eleven?" queried the first invader, consulting the tab of a key.

"I can't remember," I said huffily. "I'm asleep."

"So'll we all be, pretty soon," said the second one.

By now I was fully awake. "Is this some sort of dormitory?" I asked indignantly.

"You bet," said the third, disgorging a ukulele from the inside of one of the elephants which, now that I could focus, turned out to be very large rucksacks. The others, meanwhile, had thrown their elephants on the floor and were sitting on the other beds trying to take off their socks. The socks appeared to be fighting back.

"Jeese," said one. "Some ape's left a bicycle in here."

"It's mine," I said hastily.

"Oh. You mean you *ride* that thing? Looks more like a kid's bike to me."

"It's a lovely bike," I said protectively. "And if you don't mind, I think I'll try to get back to sleep. I've had rather a long day." I pulled the bed-cover over my head and lay listening to the invaders cleaning their teeth; I really was terribly tired, and I'd just dropped off again when someone shook my shoulder.

"Pardon me, but would you mind moving?"

I threw back the bed-cover and sat up.

"Yes, I would mind. I'd mind very much."

"Only to another bed. That one over there." A hand waved in the direction of what appeared to be a toddler's cot in the corner of the room.

"Why should I?" It seemed to me that the time had come for me to stand up for my rights.

"Well, it's like this. You're in the biggest bed, and. . . ."

I suddenly became aware that there were now four extra people in the room, instead of three, and that the window of the room was wide open. Somebody, obviously, hadn't got enough cash to pay for a separate bed. Groaning feebly, I crawled out of the big bed, revealing my glamorous nightwear—the navy singlet and gym knickers—and staggered to the cot in the corner. I can't think how I fitted myself in, but I was still there when I woke up the next morning.

The invaders had vanished. The only sign that they had ever been there was the neatly-folded sheets piled on the ends of the beds and, tied to Daisy's handlebars, a half-eaten chocolate bar with the words "Have a good day" scribbled on the wrapper.

The sun was shining and the air was crisp as I pedalled off down the parkway. On one side of the road, an inlet of the Atlantic sparkled like a jeweller's shop window; on the other, trees in full blossom cascaded down green slopes, tossing breeze-borne petals over the tarmac. Birds sang cheerily from every bush. I had never, in a single morning, seen so many birds that I didn't know, and had to stop continually to consult my pocket birdbook.

What was that little green bird, wearing what looked like a schoolboy's red cap? It had the impressive name of ruby-

crowned kinglet. And the one that resembled a large iridescent
blackbird? A purple grackle. Robins as big as English thrushes,
cerulean warblers, yellow-throated warblers, zebra-striped wood-
peckers . . . I was so fascinated by the birds that I didn't notice
that I was leaving the open woodlands lining the sea-shore and
was plunging into a dark inland forest. The trees thickened
along the roadside and the view of the sea vanished; now and
again a car passed me, and occasionally a dog barked forlornly in
the distance, but where, I wondered, was the next village? I got
out my map.

That must be where I was—about 15 miles from Charles City.
It sounded a good place to stop, Charles City—there'd probably
be a couple of motels and some nice restaurants. I pedalled on
hopefully.

At length I came to a cross-roads in the forest. A small general
store, looking distinctly run-down, stood in one of the angles of
the roads, and in two of the others there were apparently-
deserted shacks. The fourth angle was empty except for two
recumbent dogs, both of which were too lethargic even to raise
their heads as I approached.

I went into the store. Flies were crawling over the shelves and
the liquid in the soft-drinks bottles had separated into layers of
what looked like scum topped with water. Cautiously, I chose a
piece of foil-wrapped cheese.

"How far is it to Charles City?" I asked, paying my bill.

The old lady behind the cash register looked at me with suspicion. "You're in Charles City," she announced, pushing my
change towards me and quickly withdrawing her hand, as if concerned that I might touch her.

"How far to the next town, then?"

She shrugged her shoulders, as if to indicate that not only did
she not know, but that she was totally uninterested as well. Feeling that I might worry her if I picnicked near her store, I
pedalled on for about a mile and then, as I wolfed down the
cheese, studied my map again. There seemed to be a town only
a few miles further on.

But when I got to where the town ought to have been, all I found was a school and a petrol station. The latter had a CLOSED sign hung on its single pump, and from the former a child-laden school bus was just being driven away. A teacher came out, locking the door behind him.

"Please!" I cried. "Is there anywhere round here I could spend the night? Or get a meal?" I'd never before seen a school set down in the middle of nowhere—surely there must be a village somewhere around.

"I'd try Richmond, if I was you," said the teacher, getting into his car.

"How far is it?" I asked, clinging rather desperately to the edge of his still-open door.

"Oh . . . only about 30 miles." He slammed the door and drove off.

Thirty miles? But the sun was almost setting, and even if it hadn't been I couldn't have mustered the strength to pedal that far. I watched the teacher's car bounce off down the road, and looked round for a place to put up my tent.

It was very eerie, sleeping near that empty school—the chains of the playground swings rattled in the dark like the fetters of some recaptured runaway slave, and near midnight the wind caught the school bell, making it toll like Edgar Allan Poe's,

> Keeping time, time, time,
>   In a sort of Runic rhyme,
> To the tintinnabulation that so musically wells
>   From the bells, bells, bells, bells.

Poe, incidentally, although born in Boston, spent much of his early nineteenth-century childhood in Virginia.

That night by the school I formulated my second rule, to join the one already made about always carrying food. This second rule read Never Rely on a Name, and was sub-titled If the Mapmakers Call it Megalopolis, that Means it's Only Got One Tap. From then on, I didn't rely on any "town" having a food store, let alone a motel.

VIRGINIA (1)

The next day I was deep in the heart of Virginia, heading north towards Richmond. Richmond—which had been the capital of the Confederacy during the 1861-5 Civil War—sounded such a romantic town that I half expected it to be full of pretty girls in crinolines; it was, instead, rather disappointingly peopled by men in normal city suits.

Clear of Richmond, I went into stud-farming country. Stable buildings as neat as toy-shop farms were ringed by paddocks as well-tended as vicarage lawns; white fences gleamed as if they had been painted only days before, and the large frame houses—surrounded by trees that would not have disgraced a ducal park—bore every sign of being their owners' pride and joy. Between the precisely-spaced glazing bars the glass of the windows gleamed with polish, and on the roofs not a solitary shingle was out of place. Shining-coated thoroughbreds—some of them mares with foals—munched contentedly on the astonishingly green grass.

It was still April, and the previous evening I had found my tent distinctly cold; the more I thought about it the more entranced I became with the idea of spending at least one night snuggled up in a cosy barn. As the sun began to go down I knocked on the imposing-looking door of one of the stud-farm houses.

"Please, could I spend the night in your barn? I'd be awfully careful." And, remembering what a horror all farmers have of fire, I added, "I don't smoke."

The sun-tanned girl who had opened the door smiled welcomingly.

"Come in, come in. We're just sitting down to dinner. Care to join us?"

I wasn't yet entirely used to the Americans' hospitality towards strangers, and when after dinner the girl and her husband tried to get me to accept their offer of a bed I was adamant.

"No, no—the meal was really great, but I couldn't dream of landing myself on you for the night. I'll be quite all right in the barn. Honestly."

I thought the husband looked a little puzzled as he shepherded me across the yard.

"Are you sure you'll be OK?" he asked anxiously.

"Oh yes, absolutely. Good night—and many thanks again for everything."

He strode away, swinging his lantern, while I shone my pocket torch around the inside of the barn. To my horror, I saw none of the comforting straw that I had been expecting. Some American horses, it seems, are bedded down on a mixture of sawdust and bark-chippings that is delivered in polythene sacks about the size and consistency of tar barrels. I think I'd have had a better night tucked up with a posse of performing seals.

That night in the barn taught me lesson number three, which was Look Before You Lie. From then on, I never assumed that a place would be comfortable just because it sounded as if it ought to be, and always had a look before committing myself. True, before the end of the trip I slept in some pretty strange places, but at least I never again put up with unsatisfactory shelter if there was any possibility of something better. After all, as the original Chief Scout once said, any fool can be uncomfortable.

The next morning I crept off at dawn, leaving a thank-you note pinned to the barn door. It was a bit difficult to know what to say without actually fibbing, so I thanked them again for

their hospitality and simply said that it had been a night that I
would long remember.

A low mist was hanging over the fields, but already every bird
in Virginia seemed to be singing its head off in preparation for
the rising of the sun, which suddenly shot over the horizon,
whisking away the mist. All around me, as I bicycled, the farms
came to life. Tractor engines coughed, coughed, coughed again
and then hummed in a self-important way; dogs barked inquir-
ingly, and children stood sleepy-eyed at gates, waiting for the
school bus. A postman passed, driving an ordinary car with a
sticker on it saying "U.S. MAIL," and flicking up the signal-flags
on the road-side delivery-boxes as he popped in letters for the
distant houses. From paddock to paddock, horses whinnied encouragingly to each other, and from beyond a grassy hillock
came the querulous bray of a waking donkey.

I stopped at a wooden bridge and climbed down to the stream
below. The water was ice-cold, and so clear that I could see each
golden pebble on the bed of the stream. As I splashed the water
on my face the lingering tiredness of the previous night
vanished; I scooped up some of the water in my billycan and sat
on the parapet of the bridge, sipping the water between bites of
a dried-up sandwich that I had saved from the day before. I don't
think I've ever enjoyed a breakfast more in all my life.

Another long day's bicycling westwards and I had left the
stud farms and was into an area of rather poor-looking small-
holdings. The wind blew steadily into my face and I found the
going very, very hard. As Daisy had only three gears, any sizeable
hill forced me to get off and walk; I must have walked almost as
many miles as I biked, and my feet got extremely sore. Towards
evening, on a deserted bit of road, I lay down with them stuck
up on a bank, to give them a good rest.

Suddenly, I realised that a helicopter, which had passed over a
few moments before, had come back and was hovering over me
like a hungry hawk. I couldn't really flatter myself that it was
the beauty of my legs—sticking out from my rolled-up jeans—
that had bewitched the pilot, so what could it be? Then I

realised that as I'd dropped Daisy into the ditch, and was lying with my head in the road and my feet stuck up on the bank, it must have looked—from the air—as if I'd had a nasty accident. I sprang up hastily, did a little dance, and waved to the pilot, who gave a bounce of acknowledgment and then swiftly buzzed off.

I turned up a rough track and knocked at the door of the small wooden house that stood, surrounded by broken-down farm buildings, a little way off the road. The door opened a fraction, and an elderly black face, its cheeks peppered with several days' growth of grey whiskers, peered out.

"I'm so sorry to disturb you, but I wonder if I could camp in one of your fields?"

The old man stared at me then, without saying a word, shut the door. No luck, I thought, turning Daisy and starting to wheel her back to the road. I was just about to mount when I heard a shout behind me.

"Hey. Ma'am!"

I turned and saw a fat black woman hastening down the path towards me. She was wearing a button-fronted cotton dress— each button strained to the utmost—and the front part of her hair was wound round outsize pink plastic rollers.

"Ma'am . . . was you wanting something?"

"I'm looking for somewhere to camp."

"That's what my Pa said. But I just couldn't imagine. . . ." She hesitated, rubbing the palms of her hands down the sides of her dress.

"Really, it doesn't matter. I can easily go a bit further."

"No, don't you do that. We'll be happy to have you stop."

I had really wanted to put up my tent in a field that I'd spotted about a hundred yards from the house, but she insisted that I should pitch it close to the back door, between a wire chicken-run and an old car tyre which, dangling from a tree-branch, evidently served as a children's swing.

"You care to join us for supper? The children'll be home presently."

Laughing and shouting, four children tore round the end of the house, stopping in their tracks when they saw me.

"Come and say how'd'y'do to our guest, kids. Ma'am, this is Duke, he's eight . . . and Luther, he's seven . . . and Marilyn, she's nine . . . and Jacqueline. Jacqueline, you're six, aren't you? Jacqueline, what are you doing, just standing there? Come and shake hands. Properly, now."

Four warm little black hands were pressed shyly into mine.

"Now you-all run and get washed up—supper'll be directly." The children made loud splashing noises in the kitchen sink, peeping out of the window and giggling excitedly.

The house was very small. The living-room, which was also the kitchen, took up most of the ground floor; it was dominated by a cumbersome old-fashioned refrigerator, and the table, which took up most of one wall, was covered with a worn plastic-coated cloth. Two tiny rooms led off the living-room; one appeared to be some sort of scullery and the other was almost entirely filled by a white-counterpaned double bed. Stairs led upwards from the alcove that sheltered the front door; judging from the angle of the roof, the rooms upstairs must have been hardly larger than cupboards. I couldn't see any sort of bathroom, and there was no shade over the electric bulb that hung, circled by a few lethargic flies, from the centre of the whitewashed ceiling. Over the unlit fireplace hung a coloured photograph of President Kennedy, behind which someone had tucked a sprig of plastic fern.

We had beans for supper, and some white bread, washed down with scalding—but very weak—coffee. I found some oranges in my rucksack, to act as dessert, and after we'd done the washing-up—which didn't take long, since we had each only used one plate—I suddenly realised that the whole family was just sitting there, staring at me. Clearly, it was up to me to provide the cabaret. I asked the children if they'd like to play a game.

"Football!" shouted Duke. I might have known it.

"Have a heart—I've been biking all day. Isn't there something we could play sitting down?"

The children glanced at each other and giggled; clearly, sitting-down games didn't play a large part in their scheme of things. I tried again.

"How about noughts and crosses?"

More giggles, from which I gathered that they'd never even heard of it. We had several hilarious games, only slightly hampered by the fact that we all had to play with a single stumpy pencil, the lead of which kept breaking.

It was dark by the time the children were sent to bed. I said good night all round, and, accomplishing the difficult feat of undressing inside my tent, wriggled into my sleeping-bag. Just as I was snuggling down I heard a little scratching sound on the fabric of the tent door. At first I thought it was one of the bumbling insects that had pestered me on previous nights, but then I heard a quickly-suppressed giggle. I unzipped the tent door, surprising Luther, who had evidently been trying to peer through the teeth of the zipper.

"Now, Luther—that's not very polite, is it?" I whispered. I didn't want to get him into trouble with his mother, who would, I felt sure, have walloped him if she'd known what he was up to.

Marilyn's face appeared alongside Luther's.

"Can we come in?" she asked hopefully.

"No, you can't."

"Why not?"

"There's no room."

"Oh yes there is—there's lots of room."

She proved her point by diving head-first into the tent and crawling quickly down towards my feet, closely followed by Jacqueline, who was wearing what appeared to be a cotton dress of her mother's, the length of which obliged her—once she had let go of the hem—to wriggle along on her stomach. While I was trying to sort out the girls, Duke and Luther seized the chance to climb in and, zipping the door shut behind them, started what seemed to be a wrestling match.

My tent was extremely small. It was, in fact, only a few inches wider than my own shoulders, and although at the door end it

was just possible to sit up in it, it tapered towards the foot end
and was, all in all, fairly closely related to a nylon stocking. By
no stretch of the imagination was it designed to hold five people, especially when two of them were fighting each other, the
third was in danger of strangling herself with her own nightwear, and the fourth had been pushed head-first into the foot of
the tent and was obviously—unless something was done pretty
quickly—going to suffocate.

"Out, boys!" I hissed, unzipping the door and bundling Duke
and Luther unceremoniously on to the damp night grass. To my
relief I could hear heavy snores coming from the house; both
mother and grandfather were, if the noise was anything to go by,
already asleep.

"It's not fair," protested Duke, clutching at his damp little
bottom. "Why should the girls get to sleep in your tent and us
boys . . . ?"

"First of all, the girls aren't going to sleep in my tent, and
secondly, boys don't sleep with ladies."

The moment I'd said it, I could see that I'd phrased it wrong.

"Yes they do. Pa sleeps with Mommie. Every time he comes
home. He does. He *does*."

"Hush, for goodness sake. You'll wake everyone up. Boys, go
right back to bed this very instant, or I'll tell your mother in the
morning. You too, girls."

I dragged Jacqueline out by the hem of her outsize nightie
and then heaved Marilyn out by her feet.

"Bed, girls," I ordered as firmly as it was possible to do without raising my voice. Reluctantly, they all trooped back into the
house. Moments later, the four of them were hanging out of an
upstairs window, whispering and throwing down lumps of the
moss that sprouted in one of the nearby gutters. I fell asleep to
the plop-plop sound of damp moss hitting the roof of my tent.

Very early the next morning, I was woken by what sounded
like a rusty fire-alarm; I clutched my ears, realising after a moment that it was only a cock, crowing in the nearby chicken-run.
I tried to turn over, and thought at first that I must have stowed

my gear badly, for something seemed to be pressing against my
back. I turned my head and saw, resting trustfully on the folded
sweater that I was using as a pillow, the little black face of
Jacqueline. Her thumb was stuck firmly in her mouth and she
was fast, fast asleep, her toes tucked neatly under a corner of my
sleeping-bag.

How she had got back in without waking me I couldn't imagine, but I picked her up carefully and tiptoed towards the house.
Luckily the door was unfastened and when I put her down beside the other children in the upstairs bedroom nobody—least of
all Jacqueline herself—woke up.

I sent the children small presents from the next town that I
reached—Charlottesville—but after I'd tied up the parcel I had
to undo it again to add something that I'd forgotten—a box of
coloured pencils, for playing noughts and crosses.

VIRGINIA (2)

I would have liked to linger in Charlottesville, which lay south of Washington. Its university, opened in 1825, had been Thomas Jefferson's favourite architectural project—dominated by a modified version of the Pantheon in Rome—and it seemed an altogether delightful town. But I was getting a little worried, for although I had been bicycling hard for nearly a week I hadn't yet got out of Virginia—the very first state on my itinerary. Ahead of me still lay—if I stuck to my planned route—Kentucky, Illinois, Missouri, Kansas, Colorado, Wyoming, Montana, Idaho and Oregon. And if I was going to wander off my route (as indeed I did) there would be even more states to cross. I really had to get on, and on top of that, I needed to have a bath.

I put one foot down on a Charlottesville pavement-edge, and stopped a nice-looking couple.

"Excuse me, but would you kindly tell me which is the best hotel round here?"

I was a bit overwhelmed when the one they directed me to turned out to be a very luxurious country club. I chained Daisy to some impressive wrought-iron railings and walked into the lobby.

I knew I was looking dusty and dishevelled, so before I spoke to the reception clerk I took a deep breath and told myself firmly that I was going to ask for the best room in the place. It turned out to be a large, oak-beamed bedroom; the bed was covered with a downy quilt, and the view from the window was over a garden filled with budding roses. The bathroom had two basins, a huge bath, and more towels than I had ever seen outside a White Sale. I shook my rucksack upside-down on the floor and dumped everything that was washable into the bath; then I stripped myself naked, added the things I had been wearing, turned on the taps, shook in some detergent—and stepped in on top of the heap. For good measure, I also shampooed my hair, and by the time I went downstairs again I really looked quite respectable, especially as my voile dress, which I had packed rolled up, was in surprisingly good shape. I strolled into the discreetly lit bar, and ordered myself a drink, only to discover, too late, that I had left my purse upstairs and, what's more, couldn't remember my room number.

"No problem," said the middle-aged man at the next table. He turned to the waiter. "Include the lady's drink with my last order, will you?" He turned back to me. "Your husband can take care of it when he comes down," he added kindly.

"But I haven't got a husband. I mean, my husband's not here."

He looked faintly surprised.

"I'm travelling alone."

The surprise became tinged with just the smallest suspicion of withdrawal. I felt I needed to explain.

"I'm bicycling across America."

"You're what?"

"Bicycling across America. From the Atlantic to the Pacific."

"No kidding?" His face was creased with disbelief.

"Scout's honour."

By now several of the man's friends had joined him and I was finding myself rather flatteringly the centre of attention.

"But what made you choose to travel on a bicycle?" asked a second man.

"I wanted to see the real America," I said—and then suddenly realised how silly that sounded, considering how I was staying at what must surely have been the plushiest watering-hole for miles around. All the men were in dinner-jackets and the women were wearing obviously expensive jewellery. "That is, I mean. . . ," I stumbled on. We all had dinner together. Filet Mignon, Chateau Latour, Soufflé Grand Marnier.

I got up early the next morning, and finished drying my clothes by turning the air-conditioning unit up to maximum. A few golfers were already out on the club's private course, and a couple of track-suited joggers were battling their way round the perimeter of the lake; but there was no sign of my acquaintances of the previous night, so leaving a farewell note with the hall porter I unchained Daisy and set off down the road.

Ahead of me now lay the first really picturesque part of my route—the Appalachian mountains. These run roughly from Canada down to Georgia, and I was going to strike them about half-way down, approximately—on European terms—on a level with Athens. I never ceased to be surprised at how far south the United States lies. If one comes from England one tends to think that it's on about the same latitude as the British Isles, and I was amazed to find that, in bicycling roughly across the middle of it, by far the greater part of my trip was going to be done on a level with the Mediterranean, and that even the most northerly "leg"—up into Montana—would only bring me to the latitude of central France.

The first ridge of the Appalachians, which I reached after a hard ride from the country club, had a road running along its crest. Looking back from this, I could see mile after mile of hills receding, in a hundred gradations of blue, towards the plain across which I'd just bicycled. Pines and birches and other upland trees gave the scenery much the appearance of Scotland, but the state camping-ground that I stumbled on was very different to those that I had seen at home. To begin with there were proper sites for tents—not just areas of grass on which they could be pitched, but a definite site for each tent, ringed with a narrow stone-filled trench to keep out surface water, and provided with benches and a wooden table for meals. Caravans were given individual tarmac bays, set at discreet distances from each other and connected by winding roads; there were clean lavatories and basins with hot water, housed in small log cabins that blended into the surroundings, and a lot of water-points. Each site had a stone barbecue-pit; the wood for these was free— one could collect as much as one wanted from a pile by the entrance gate.

Later that night, when the temperature dropped below freezing, I wished that I had made myself a fire. I had an air-bed to insulate my sleeping-bag from the ground, but to save weight I had only bought a half-length one, which meant that although my body was comfortable, my legs had no air-bed below them and had to rely for both comfort and insulation on whatever spare equipment I could shove under them. It was hard to decide whether to put gear under my legs or over my body; everything was pressed into service to keep the cold away—my maps went under my knees, spare inner-tubes under my calves, while the rucksack made a sort of muff for my feet. Spare clothes? On nights like these there weren't any—I had every single thing on me, and even my "best" dress was made use of; rolled into its own little voile bag, it made into a very comfortable pillow.

As usual, I had sited my tent with the opening facing east, and when I unzipped the door the next morning it was wonderful to feel the first warming rays of the sun. But later in the day, as I continued along the crest-top ridge, I was fooled by the crisp air of the altitude and didn't realise how strong the sun had become. Towards afternoon, wheeling Daisy down a precipitous hill named, rather too aptly, Vesuvius, I suddenly realised that it wasn't only my brakes that had got hot—I myself was glowing. I had got a very bad case of sunburn.

The next stretch of road took me down a long valley, lying between the Blue Ridge and the main part of the Appalachians, and as I groaned my way down it I felt that every turn of the pedals was going to flay me. I checked into a motel, and had my first glimpse of myself in a bathroom mirror. Two bloodshot eyes peered back at me from a face like a scarlet beach-ball.

Don't, if you ever get a really bad case of sunburn, let anyone persuade you to treat it with such things as calomine lotion; when it's really painful and widespread, as mine was, the only thing to do is to get into a bath full of tepid water and lie there until you think that you may—perhaps—be going to survive. If possible, get someone to feed you with cool liquid, to counteract your general dehydration; I didn't have anyone to actually feed me but an efficient Room Service routed some cans of cold beer as far as my door, and I just had the strength to pull off the tabs.

Thanks to my bath-beer treatment, I felt quite lively next morning, and as I obviously wasn't going to get better quicker by staying still than I was by pressing on, I packed away the skimpy shorts and singlet that I had worn the previous day and, easing myself gingerly into my jeans and a long-sleeved jersey, set off again.

My face was a bit of a problem, as I was convinced that if so much as a blink of sun reached it, it would all peel completely off, leaving me—so to speak—pedalling along in my skull; so I pulled my little denim hat well down over my forehead and then tied my headscarf so that it reached from my collar to my sunglasses. Dangerous Dan McGrew would have recognised me instantly as a likely recruit for his gang.

Cringing under the curious stares of passers-by and sweating profusely inside the long-sleeved jersey, I pedalled relentlessly down a road that seemed simply to go round and round under my wheels, like those sets of rollers on which people ride bicycles indoors. By lunch-time I was convinced that my jeans were lined with sand-paper and that my jersey was permanently fused to my half-flayed shoulders. Abingdon—the next dot on my map —seemed more difficult to reach than the moon.

KENTUCKY

By now, quite a lot of Americans had told me how silly they thought I was, to be bicycling alone across the States; out of politeness, they used the word "brave," but it was quite clear what they really meant. But I could never, myself, see anything to be frightened of.

There were, however, some areas of the States that I felt a little apprehensive about. One was the Appalachian mountains, the main range of which was now right ahead, and as I struggled uphill—wishing, as usual, that Daisy had got a wider set of gears —I tried to concentrate on the beauty of the scenery, and put out of my head all that I had heard about coal-trucks. The drivers of these trucks, it seemed, were all on piece-work, which meant that the more trips they did each day, the more money they took home; they were reputed to show no mercy to other road-users, and as the Appalachian area was full of coal—and consequently of coal-trucks—rumour had it that only mad dogs and Englishmen would take a bicycle anywhere near it.

I tried, as a precaution, to buy a fanny-bumper. This, I had read, was a fluorescent orange circle fixed to a belt which one wore round one's waist, so as to be easily seen by people wanting to overtake, but none of the shops I tried had even heard of it, so I settled for an orange hunting hat, pensioning off the blue denim one I had started with. This new hat had a sort-of band at the back, that could either be tucked up or let down to cover one's ears, and eyelets at the side which were—the salesman told me—to allow my scalp to breathe. It kept on blowing off, so I sewed on a loop of elastic, like the ones on the St. Trinian panamas; after that, when it blew off it snapped back, making a frustrated sort of twang.

The Cumberland Gap—the pass over which many of the early settlers had slogged their way to the west—was now a six-lane highway, and I headed for a smaller pass, lying to the north. There, the foothills of the Appalachians were very peaceful. Clear mountain streams gurgled through meadows of a picture-book greenness; coppices of alders, aspens and birches—each branch hazed with opening buds—draped themselves over hills as rounded and rural-looking as cottage loaves. The village store where I stopped to buy food was crowded with good-natured loungers, cutting themselves hunks of cheese and flipping the metal caps off soft-drink bottles. When it was time to leave each customer mentioned casually to the store-owner what it was that he had taken, and sometimes money passed, and sometimes it didn't; neither side seemed in the least concerned, either one way or the other.

In defiance of everything that I had been told about not camping next to streams—because of the danger of flash floods— I spent my first Appalachian night in a water-meadow. The buttercups were growing so closely together that it was impossible to pitch my tent without crushing at least a hundred, and as I slipped into sleep the stream babbled softly, like the voice of a child confiding secrets to another child in a darkened nursery. When I awoke, each half-opened buttercup cradled a glinting diamond of dew.

Bicycling on in the golden early-morning light, I passed a sign saying WELCOME TO KENTUCKY; at last I was out of Virginia.

I climbed higher and higher, the pretty meadows and copses gradually giving way to sparser fields and thicker woods. I was just congratulating myself on reaching what I felt sure must be the watershed when the first coal-truck appeared. Horn blaring, it tore down the narrow road towards me, lumps of coal hurtling off its back like sparks flying from a Catherine wheel. There wasn't possibly room for both of us on the road. And behind me there was just a wall of rocks. "SLOW DOWN," I howled helplessly as I flattened Daisy against the stones at my back. The lorry crashed past, so close that the displaced air hit me like the blast from an exploding bomb. Shaking, I got Daisy back on to the road and wobbled onwards, my eardrums painfully taut as I listened for the arrival of other trucks.

Soon I began to recognise the noise of a truck's approach. It was a sort of horrendous banging, like a shelf-full of giant saucepans crashing into a Brobdingnagian sink, but sometimes even this horrible racket got masked by the noise of other cars, and a coal-truck would be on top of me before I had time to get off the road. Frantically, I would pedal to reach a point of escape before it got me—it wasn't enough merely to stand aside, I had to be right in the ditch if I wasn't to be scraped by those enormous metal flanks. And, gruesomely, the trucks seemed to be driven by men without faces—the drivers so caked with coal-dust that only the whites of their eyes showed under their tin hats.

"Hi!" said a girl, pulling up an ancient pick-up truck beside me, as I slouched on the edge of the road. "You look all tuckered out. Like a ride?"

"Oh yes please—I'd really love it." I was so pulverised with a combination of fright and exhaustion that I could barely heave Daisy on to the back of the truck. The girl watched me, swivelling round in the driving seat; she looked faintly amused, as if the notion of anyone being so weak was rather quaint. I climbed in beside her.

"Where'you going?" she queried amiably, letting in the clutch. Her bare foot, pressed on the disintegrating rubber of the pedal, had pale grooves where sweat had run down between her toes: the rest of her foot was the colour of the floor of the truck, which was, in turn, the colour of the road.

"Oh, just sort of this way," I answered vaguely. It didn't seem quite the right moment to say that I was heading for Oregon.

"Not goin' down the valley?" the girl asked, glancing at me sharply. "They won't let y' in, y' know. The military—they've sealed the whole pitch off."

"Why's that?"

The girl crashed the gears, swore, found the right one, and accelerated recklessly round a blind corner.

"Floods. Jes' terrible. Folks has lost everything. Say, mind if I stop off for some groceries?"

She pulled up, brakes grinding, at a tin-roofed building. It seemed to be not only a general store but also a garage; the ground in front of it was littered with discarded engine parts, and an upturned oil drum was spilling its dregs into the dust around the door.

"Anythin' you need?" inquired the girl, as I followed her round. The shelves were stacked with the usual assortment of tinned foods, breakfast cereals, candy bars and wilting vegetables. I picked up some small essentials and then, with some sort of premonition, added a large tin of ham.

"Where'you plannin' to stop the night?" Groceries thrown in the back of the truck, we were jolting off down the road.

"Anywhere, really. I'm camping."

"Can't camp around here," said the girl firmly. "Ain't safe. Might get more rain."

The weather had turned grey, and it was appreciably colder. The forest, too, looked somehow different—we were going downhill, with a small river on one side and a steep hillside on the other, and the trees near the river seemed to have a lot of dead foliage on their branches. Suddenly I saw that it wasn't all dead foliage—why, twenty feet above the ground there was a dog-kennel, lodged in the branches of a spruce, and further on, hanging upside-down from the crook of an oak, was what appeared to be a chest of drawers.

"See what I mean?" said the girl, peering out through the dusty windscreen and indicating with a bitten-nailed finger a caravan that was lying on its side in the river-bed. "Quite a storm, it was."

A couple of miles further on she pulled up at an almost-invisible side-road.

"This is where I turn off. Care to camp up at our place? It's good and high—right away from the river. Suit yourself," she added, as if not wanting to put on any pressure.

"I'd be glad to—that is, if you're sure it wouldn't be any trouble."

As soon as I saw the farm at the top of that rough side-road, I knew that this wasn't a family that bothered much about trouble. Nobody had troubled to mend the porch steps, so that the crowd of children who piled out of the house as the truck drove up had to jump from the porch floor to the ground to avoid putting their feet through the rotten treads. Naturally, nobody troubled to introduce anybody to anybody, and I just had to work out on my own who was who.

The children, whom nobody had troubled to wash for quite a time, scrambled into the back of the truck and started digging in the grocery box.

"Stop that, now! Get all that stuff out!" ordered the girl. A packet of bacon fell from the back of the truck on to the hard earth of the yard and split open; instantly, a flock of hens hastened up and began to scratch and peck.

"Now see what you've done," reprimanded the girl, not sounding in the least upset. "Shoo! Shoo!" The hens retreated, cackling loudly, as she picked up the slices of bacon, gave them a perfunctory shake, and threw them back into the grocery box.

"Take it in," she commanded, grabbing the biggest boy as he jumped off the back of the truck. "And tell Gran we've got a visitor."

An elderly lady came out of the house, wiping her hands on a T-shirt tied by its arms round her waist; it was printed with a mauve-on-yellow representation of Elvis Presley's face, the chin dragged askew by a rip in the fabric. Steadying herself on one of the poles that supported the roof of the porch, she stepped carefully down the broken steps and came towards me, smiling broadly. Her open mouth seemed to have only two teeth, both brown and broken, and the hand that she extended to me was set in a rigid, arthritic claw.

"Glad to meet you."

"Me too. What a beautiful view you've got here."

"Like livin' in a picture," said the old lady proudly. "Jes' like livin' in a picture."

We stood looking at the panorama of trees and tiny meadows that fell away in front of the house. Each pine seemed to have been placed with the care of a Capability Brown, and the spring green of the birches stood out with feathery clarity against the haze of distant hills. On an unfenced triangle of grass a tethered cow browsed amid a profusion of mountain flowers and near her, where a length of galvanised pipe poured a miniature half-rainbow of water into a small pond, a family of ducklings splattered like wind-up Christmas toys. As if on cue, a flight of barn swallows wheeled in over the birches, hawked briefly above our heads and then, with a flick of blue-black wings and pinky-buff undersides, vanished over the valley. The old lady watched them, smiling.

The house seemed only marginally larger than the one I'd visited in Virginia. Again, there was only one main room downstairs, but this time the sink and stove were in a lean-to kitchen at the back. The second downstairs room was tiny—hardly more than a cupboard, and standing just inside it was a pretty, fair-haired girl wearing a blue nylon slip and grubby feather-trimmed bedroom slippers. She made no attempt to shut the door.

"Hi! I'm Geraldine. Where'you from?"

I had got used to this direct question—it was the first one that everybody asked me.

"England."

"England?" She sounded incredulous; most people did, once I was off the tourist routes. "Say, d'you really have castles, and all that jazz?"

A horn sounded raucously in the yard.

"Hell," said the girl, not waiting for an answer about the castles. "Tell him I'll be out in a mo'." She turned, and started hunting among some dresses that were hanging on a rail behind her.

The old lady had gone through to the kitchen, where she was unpacking the groceries with the girl who had brought me, so I put my ham-tin down on the table and went out to give the message. A young man with a metal safety helmet pushed to the back of his head was leaning out of a very dusty Chevrolet; as I came out, he started banging the panel of the car door with the flat of his hand.

"Come on, come on," he yelled. "And see if Ella'll come too. Frieda's sick." He looked at me, suddenly realising that he was talking to a stranger.

"Shall I tell someone?"

"I'd be obliged." He lit a cigarette, tucking the spent match carefully back into the box. I went through to the kitchen.

"The man out there, he says Frieda's sick and can Ella come?"

"Like hell I'll come," said the girl who'd brought me, straightening up from a battered corner cupboard, where she was stacking some tins of condensed milk. "Eight hours behind a gas pump and now he wants me to wash dishes."

"Please, Ella," said the man, coming into the kitchen behind me. He held his cigarette cupped in his hand, the burning end pointing backwards into his palm. "Please. Pay night. You know how it is."

"I said no, didn't I?"

"Could I help?" I asked. "I don't know what Frieda usually does, but perhaps . . . ?"

"Dishes," said Ella. "Dishes and glasses. Three hours. Six dollars. You're welcome to it. I'll save y' a bite of supper."

Wedged between Geraldine, who had put on a low-cut dress patterned with what appeared to be a squadron of flying saucers, and the young man, who was still wearing his safety helmet, I was bounced back down the track to the main road. A couple more miles, and we turned off again, pulling up on a rough parking lot among a jumble of lorries and cars.

"This way," said Geraldine, going ahead into a large wooden hut. With booths set all along one wall, it gave the impression of an open-plan railway coach; the whole of the wall opposite the booths was taken up by a bar, behind which were big glass-doored refrigerators crammed with every sort and kind of drink. Between the booths and the bar were some tables, set roughly with thrown-down handfuls of cutlery, and at the far end of the hut a juke-box was pouring out an ear-splitting assortment of howls, thuds, bangs, crashes and screams. Apart from some low-hung lamps over the central tables, the only light came from behind the bar, and the whole place was crammed absolutely solid with men. I felt as if I'd suddenly been thrown into an old-time western saloon.

Geraldine grabbed my hand and barged gaily through the crowd.

"Shift y' bloody backside," she yelled happily at a large man who hadn't moved enough to let her through. I squeezed after her before the crowd had time to close up again. Most of the men must have come straight from work, as, even though they were indoors, they were still wearing their brightly-coloured safety helmets; many of their faces were still coated with grime, but a few had on clean checked shirts and there was even one in what looked like a technician's white cotton coat. We ducked under the bar, and went into the comparative calm of the kitchen.

A wizened little man, with a face so ashen that he might have spent all his life underground, was breaking eggs into a huge, grease-encrusted frying pan.

"She's come to help out," said Geraldine, "'stead of Frieda." Then, with a whisk of her saucy bottom, she turned back into the bar.

The old man regarded me with an expression of the utmost disgust. Then he wiped his nose on the back of his hand and resumed his expert cracking of the eggs. After a moment he jerked his head towards a corner of the kitchen.

"Over there," he said abruptly. In the corner, there was a stained, low-sided sink; it was already piled high with dirty dishes. "It's only three hours," I told myself, rolling up my sleeves.

Three hours? It felt more like three weeks. Through a hatch that connected the kitchen with the bar the old man hurled a seemingly endless line of plates piled with fried eggs, hamburgers, chips and hot dogs, and back through another hatch came an avalanche of clammy beer glasses, stained coffee cups, sticky cutlery, and plates larded with beer-can rings, spat-out food and cigarette butts.

Even if I had fallen head-first into the sink and drowned I don't think anyone would have taken a blind bit of notice, they were all having such a good time—the customers were having a good time, drinking and eating and shouting jokes at each other, and Geraldine and the other pretty girls who worked behind the bar were having the best time of all, laughing and teasing and—at frequent intervals—slipping tips into the pockets of their frilly little aprons.

Late in the evening, we dropped off the other girls at a caravan park and jolted back up the hill to the farm. The young man had—at last—taken off his safety helmet and cleaned up his face revealing himself as a likely candidate for the title of Mr. America. Geraldine, snuggled up against him on the front seat, kept on kissing him, which didn't much surprise me; the only thing that did surprise me was that the car ever got back to the top of the hill, because as far as I could make out he was steering it with his knees.

I toppled out of the back seat and groped my way into the house. I hadn't been able to face eating while I was washing up and now I was greatly looking forward to the supper that Ella had said she'd leave for me. But when I found the light switch, the unshaded bulb only illuminated two small cats, sitting on

the table licking round the inside of the empty ham-tin. There
didn't seem to be anything else.

I tottered out again, located my rucksack, and set about
finding a flat bit of ground on which to pitch my tent. But
within groping distance of that house all the ground went either
up, or down, or was covered with boulders, so in the end I just
laid my sleeping-bag out on the porch, and fell asleep to the
murmur of giggles from the parked Chevrolet.

I awoke to see the sky paling behind the black outlines of the
tree-covered hills. The Chevrolet had gone. For once I was feeling deliciously warm and, stretching out a hand, I found that
the cats had curled up in the crook of my knees.

I lay tickling them behind their ears, thinking about the globe
on which I was lying. Twenty-four thousand eight hundred and
ninety-nine miles round the equator—that meant that, with the
earth rotating once every twenty-four hours, someone on the
equator would be travelling round at about 1,000 miles an hour.
And at the pole, zero. So if I was roughly half-way between
equator and pole, I must be going at about half the speed of
someone on the equator.

Warm and happy, two little cats and I cuddled each other on
a porch in Kentucky and, serenaded by the dawn chorus of
myriad birds, spun at 500 miles an hour towards the rising
sun.

KENTUCKY AND MISSOURI

"Goodbye! Goodbye!" yelled everyone as I wheeled Daisy down the track. "Come back and see us!"

The household had grown since the previous evening, and as well as the grandmother, the two girls, and the children, there was an unidentified man, another woman, and a baby all gathered on the porch to see me off. The baby, though he didn't know it, was richer by six dollars—my earnings of the night before, which I'd tucked down the side of his broken-down pram.

"Goodbye! Thanks for everything!" I turned as I reached the main road, for a last look at the little farm, but it was already lost behind the trees.

Moments after Daisy's wheels struck the main road I realised that this wasn't going to be an easy day. Riding in the Chevrolet the previous evening I hadn't noticed that at this level the valley was larded with a sort of sludge. The high-water mark of the flood had been far above the surface of the road, and when the water retreated the silt that it had left behind had coated the surface of the tarmac like soft icing on a cake; in places, this had dried to a rutted consistency, like giant corrugated paper, and where bulldozers had scraped it into the ditches great round potholes—where the swirling flood-water had corkscrewed large lumps of asphalt out of the surface of the road—forced me to zigzag like a skier negotiating a slalom. Soon, giving up the struggle, I got off and walked; this turned out to be rather lucky, because I slipped unnoticed past the checkpoints where the soldiers were stopping cars.

As I dropped further and further down the valley, the devastation grew. Complete areas were swept clear of houses; cars, caravans, furniture and other debris were piled higgledy-piggledy against anything that had impeded the rush of the flood-water; uprooted trees embraced ones that were still standing, forming huge log-jams of trunks and tangled branches. The weather had turned suddenly hot, and steam rose everywhere, like smoke from a forest fire. A strange smell filled the air—sweet but somehow repulsive, like fermenting jam.

"When did it happen?" I asked a man who was dejectedly shovelling the rotting contents of a freezer into plastic sacks.

"Six days ago."

"Six days?" What, I wondered, could things have been like on the day that it actually happened?

At the mouth of the valley, where the mountains finally opened out into the plain, stood the remains of the town that had received the final, pent-up fury of the flood. Fire-engines were pumping up water from the now-calm river, in an attempt to wash the silt from houses and streets. Furniture and ruined goods of every sort were stacked in the parks, in the playgrounds, and on the pavements. Some shops were open, their soaking, mud-sodden stock heaped in dripping piles on the highest of their counters, but most, although their doors stood ajar, were not doing any trading. Instead their owners, with dirt-caked brooms, were battling to sweep debris out into the streets, where bulldozers were shifting the wreckage into manageable heaps. Everywhere there were soldiers, alert, freshly laundered, decisive, sharply contrasting with the civilians who—understandably—still looked in a state of shock.

The only restaurant that was open was jammed to the doors; the people who couldn't get in just stood in the street, munching the hamburgers that their friends inside had passed to them; in a small park, a long queue snaked away from a mobile field kitchen.

I cleared the silt from the bonnet of an abandoned car and spread out the contents of my food bag—clearly, there would be no point in trying to help if I was, at the same time, going to make demands on the town's resources of food. I had an orange, some instant coffee, half a packet of biscuits, and a small jar of peanut butter. Even as I looked, the peanut butter started to turn oily in the hot sun; the change had a sinister effect, like the speeded-up disintegration of a horror-film corpse.

Nearby, there was a chemist's shop. The water must have invaded it to about eye-level, for the lower half of the front window had a curtain of dried silt brushed across it, so that I had to stand on tip-toe to see into the interior. At first I thought that the shop was empty, then from behind one of the counters a man appeared. He was lifting up a packing-carton; laboriously he rose to his feet, walked leadenly to the door, and threw the carton into the gutter. Tins of baby-food burst from the sodden cardboard; the mud, as though it had been molten lava, engulfed them instantly.

"Can I help?"

"Naw. I'm OK."

"Please—I've nothing else to do."

The man looked at me in a way that was almost suspicious.

"You a pharmacist?"

"No."

"But you can read?"

For a second I thought he was simply being rude; then I saw the point of his question.

"Mind if I bring my bike in?" I asked.

For the rest of the day, I stood over a plastic baby-bath, washing his stock. Anything that the water had got into, or which had had its label washed off, had to be thrown out, but first whatever was in the bottle or jar had to be tipped into a rubbish-sack, to avoid even the slightest chance that a dangerous drug might go astray. In the dirty street, I jumped up and down on a plastic sack filled with thousands of brightly-coloured pills; they crackled and popped under my feet like daemonic breakfast-food.

By lunch-time the following day we had done all the drugs, and were starting on the toothpaste, the hair-brushes, the nursery toys, the soap, the camera films, and all the other oddments of a modern chemist's shop. Ironically, the goods that had come out best were the cosmetics; after a flood, it seemed, one might not be able to find a clean bandage but one could be pretty sure of retaining the option, for one's lipstick, of Cherrywood, Fresh Ginger, Country Blush, Field Heather or Undeniable Pink. From inside a damaged plastic box of cosmetics the photograph of a beautiful girl peered out at me, like the face of a child pressed to the window of a car that is being driven past the scene of a crash; heartlessly I chucked her on to the rubbish-pile.

By late afternoon I was exhausted. I had already spent one night sleeping in a chair and I knew that if I did the same again I would be too tired to be of use the next day. Also, I had finished my food. I felt that the most useful thing I could do next was to get out, before I became a liability. There was a bus leaving at dusk, and I bought myself a ticket.

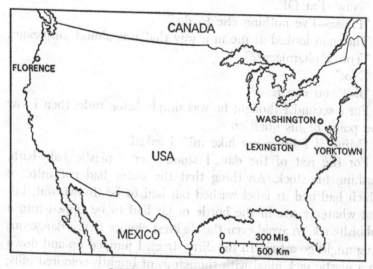

LEXINGTON, KENTUCKY

That was how I came to arrive in Lexington, the next town on my route, at midnight on the eve of the Kentucky Derby. Racing enthusiasts had booked every hotel room in the city; I roamed the dark streets—deserted except for sinister figures lurking in doorways—vainly searching for somewhere to sleep. The bag that held my money and documents was hanging over my shoulder; apprehensively, I unzipped my anorak and with difficulty tucked the bag across my stomach, where it would be out of sight; the darkened shop-windows reflected a pregnant penguin, flapping along the pavements on plimsoll feet. I waddled into what seemed to be the last hotel in the town and leant, exhausted, on the reception desk.

"Sorry, ma'am—we've been fully booked for weeks."

I couldn't go out on to those dark streets again.

"Please—I'm really scared. Please—what shall I do?"

He gave me one of the staff bedrooms. It was small and hot and the bed hadn't been made, but it was indoors, and safe, and I'll remember that compassionate reception clerk as long as I live.

The next day dawned bright and beautiful. The streets looked about as menacing as the ones in Disneyland, and were peopled with fresh-faced young men distributing religious tracts. I went back to the bus depot, where I had left Daisy the night before; sitting opposite me over breakfast in the depot café was an enormous man wearing an electric-blue suit, a flat white cap with a bobble on top, and a tie painted with magenta orchids. He was the blackest man I'd ever seen—so intensely black that he positively glistened.

"And where d'you keep your gun, ma'am? In your sack or in that little pocket-book?"

I still hadn't got used to the American habit of calling a handbag a pocket-book and, concentrating on that part of his question, I failed to grasp its main content.

"Don't tell me you're travelling without a gun!" he cried, mistaking the reason for my silence.

"A gun? Good gracious—I've not got a gun."

The black man held his hands up in horror, casting some of the sugar from his doughnut over my scrambled eggs.

"No gun? But that sure is a ba-a-ad thing. No lady ought to be travellin' alone these days without no gun."

I felt I had to explain my own point of view.

"But I wouldn't know what to do with it, even if I had one. I'd be much more danger to myself than I would be to any . . . er . . . any robber."

But he wasn't convinced, and when the announcer called his bus he went off shaking his head sadly, muttering, "No gun. Oh my. No gun. Dear dear. No gun."

The hot weather that I had first noticed in the flood town had been the forerunner of an unseasonable heat-wave. By the time I was clear of the suburbs of Lexington the temperature had risen to over ninety and, my sunburn having healed, I was back to bicycling in my navy vest and gym knickers. This combination looked so like normal bicycling gear that nobody gave it a second glance, but for decency's sake I kept the skirt of my voile two-piece on top of my map-case, to slip on if I had to dismount. I had just stopped at a shop and bought a couple of cans of iced Coke when I noticed a man changing a wheel at the side of the road. He was having trouble with the jack and I thought that a cold drink might stave off what appeared to be a threatened attack of apoplexy. We sat on the grass verge, drinking out of the cans.

"It just would happen when I was going to visit with my wife —my ex-wife, that is. She'll be mad, if I keep her waiting."

"Surely she'll understand? It's not your fault, that you got a flat."

"Not my fault? Everything's my fault, where that doll's concerned."

"Why are you going to see her? I mean, if you're not married to her any more?"

"It's her birthday, that's why. I always treat her to a gift on her birthday. She picks out what she wants, and then she calls me up to come on over, so I can pay for it."

I couldn't think what to say to this, and after a moment he went on.

"She told me to bring plenty of cash this time—she says it's a real good gift."

"Doesn't her new husband mind? You buying her . . . gifts?"

"Well, her second husband didn't much like it, and her third wasn't all that easy, but this guy she's married to now, he just dotes on her. Anything that makes her happy, that's all right by him."

I thought for a moment. "You mean she's been married three times since she left you?"

"Yes indeed—and picked up some big property settlements on the way. She's a really lovely lady. Get any man she wants just by lifting her little finger. Yes sir." And he beamed with pride, like a man whose dog has just won the Supreme Championship at Crufts'. I felt I had to get this straight.

"She's married three other men, yet she still telephones you and gets you to pay for a present to her that she's chosen?"

"Yup. Wish you could see her—she's a real beauty."

It didn't seem to matter to him that she'd left him for, so far, at least three other men, and that she sounded a mercenary little baggage at that; what mattered to him, above all, was that she was good-looking, and that somewhere along the line she'd been his wife. It was the first time that I had come face to face with the American male's almost obsessive reverence for female beauty, and I was frankly astounded.

Between us we got his spare wheel fixed and I stood on the side of the road, watching him drive happily away to the reunion with his dream girl; then, remounting Daisy, I bicycled on through the pleasant, rolling countryside. Stud farms stretched away on either side of the road, their white post-and-rail fences gleaming in the bright sunshine. It was a beautiful, prosperous area; perversely, I found it almost too rich, and missed the uninhibited friendliness of some of the poorer communities that I had left behind me. I felt almost shy when knocking on these elegant doors asking for permission to camp.

I was doing much more camping on private property than I had ever expected, because although by now it was quite late in the spring none of the public camping-sites were yet officially open—they didn't, it seemed, open till the first public holiday, some time in June.

I learnt to be very wary of guard dogs—in fact, all the way across America, dogs were a problem. Slavering at the mouth, they rushed at me from gates. Doggy fangs flashed from behind flimsy fences, doggy voices were raised in blood-curdling menace. Dogs forsook warm firesides and piled-up dinner-plates in order to rush out and threaten me with evisceration. Small dogs snapped at my ankles and large dogs leapt at my throat. Frustrated dogs on chains, deprived of what they clearly looked on as a constitutional Right To Bite, set up long-distance barking systems, alerting their pals in neighbouring farms that easy prey was heading their way.

I had had a course of tetanus shots before I left home, in case I fell off and damaged myself on a grubby road, but there's no advance innoculation available for rabies and a bite from a strange American dog is a serious matter, involving lengthy tests and possibly horrendous injections into one's stomach. All in all, I was hardly keen to risk a bite.

I tried to buy one of the aerosols that American postmen use to deter dogs, but although a postman told me that there were cases of these in the post offices, nobody seemed to sell them retail, so I took to travelling with a leafy branch, a blow from which would frighten a dog without actually hurting him.

It was a long, long way from Lexington to Louisville, even though they were both in Kentucky, and even further from Louisville to St. Louis, Missouri. Between Kentucky and Missouri I even managed to fit in little bits of Indiana and Illinois, so I was feeling pretty pleased with myself by the time the tall buildings of St. Louis started rising above the horizon.

But what was that extraordinary thing, like a giant metal rainbow, rising even higher than the skyscrapers? As I pedalled nearer, it seemed to grow larger and at the same time recede, in much the same way as a real rainbow. I was so fascinated by it that I didn't notice that I'd bicycled too far into the city to be able to camp; I checked into what looked like a reasonable hotel and set out to investigate.

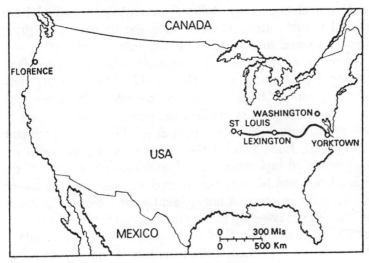

ST. LOUIS, MISSOURI

"What's that?" I asked an elderly man.

"Pardon?"

"That thing—up there."

"Some sort of blackbird, I guess. Not sure, though—my eyes ain't what they used to be."

"No, I don't mean the bird—I mean that arch thing."

"Oh that. Why, that's the Arch."

I tried again, this time asking a small boy.

"Please, would you tell me what that is?"

The child screwed up his eyes, and looked intently skywards.

"An F.15 *Eagle*," he announced decisively. "At about 20,000 feet. Armed with. . . ."

I couldn't even see the plane he was so carelessly identifying.

"No, I mean that arch."

He looked at me much as a Parisian might look at a visitor who had failed to recognise the Eiffel Tower.

"But that's the Arch," he said, turning away.

This wasn't going to get me anywhere, so I walked and walked till I reached the foot of the rainbow. It was made of stainless steel and it was taller than anything I would have believed possible; from where I stood—beside one of its giant bases—it seemed to soar quite literally into the clouds.

I went down a ramp into the enormous subterranean museum that lay buried under it. "THE GATEWAY ARCH," proclaimed a notice. "Begun in 1947 on the site of Laclede's 1764 trading post, the arch symbolizes the proud role of St. Louis in western settlement. With the 1803 acquisition of the Louisiana Territory, St. Louis became the gateway for the American nation's westward expansion. . . ." I wandered off, to look at the stuffed bison and beavers, the covered waggons and the Indian clothes in the museum. A notice said Queue Here for the Elevator. The idea of going up that monstrous croquet-hoop was most alarming, but when I looked at the people who were already in the queue—some of them quite little tots—I told myself not to be silly, and got into line. In groups of five we were marshalled into claustrophobic metal bubbles, and at an eerie angle—because of the curve of the structure—rose towards the clouds.

From the observation room at the top of the arch—with 600 feet of empty air directly beneath me—I looked over the Mississippi, studded with modern ships and the moored hulks of old paddle-steamers; on the other side lay the business area of St. Louis, containing the cupola-topped, pillared, porticoed municipal buildings common to most large American cities, the department stores, office blocks, hospitals, churches, warehouses and skyscrapers. Beyond, I could see the residential suburbs, and beyond them, the enormous plain across which I was next going to travel. From this height, it seemed so flat that I half imagined I could detect, along the furthest horizon, the curve of the surface of the world. Daisy, chained at the foot of the arch, appeared smaller than the head of a pin. If I was going to tackle that plain I wanted to start really fresh; I hadn't had so much as an afternoon without travel since I had left the flood town, and, deciding not to leave until the following morning, I took a sightseeing trip on one of those tourist buses that, had this been London, would have circled Buckingham Palace and Parliament Square. The bus was almost empty; there was a pair of elegant young men, leaning close as they adjusted each other's cameras, two middle-aged couples, three children with someone who—from their mirror-likeness to her—could only have been their mother, and five Japanese. The Japanese, sitting in the back of the bus, were too far away for me to overhear their conversation.

The bus crawled round the city, the driver making hearty jokes as he pointed out the famous breweries and not-so-famous monuments. Towards the end of the afternoon he drew up outside the botanical gardens.

"We'll take a half-hour break here," he announced. "I'm sure all you folks'll like the opportunity to visit our amazing Climatron."

We all climbed out of the bus and dutifully trooped into a vast geodetic glass-house crammed with tropical plants. Inside it was extremely hot, and I suddenly noticed that one of the Japanese was looking pale. He and I had got separated from the rest of the bus passengers, so I helped him to the door and sat him down on a convenient seat.

"Would you like a glass of water?"

He didn't seem to understand what I meant, but I thought it would do him good, so I left him on the seat and hurried into the nearby cafeteria.

"There's a man outside who's feeling faint. Could I have some water for him, please?"

The girl behind the counter filled a small paper cone.

"That'll be ten cents."

I hurried back to the bench, slopping most of the water out of the miserable little cone on the way.

"Here." The Japanese drank it, and I helped him loosen his tie. After a few minutes he began to look better.

"You wait here, and I'll see if I can find your friends."

I ducked back into the Climatron, and found the other four Japanese studying cacti.

"I'm afraid your friend isn't feeling very well. He's sitting down just outside—would you like to collect him on your way back to the bus?"

The Japanese looked at me, and then at each other.

"But we're all here," one of them said, speaking with an American accent.

"But that other gentleman—the one who was with you—I mean. . . ." I didn't quite know whether to say "Japanese" or "oriental," or what. I felt sure there must be some conventionally polite way of describing people so obviously Japanese, but I didn't know what it was.

"Oh yes, there was a tourist on the bus, wasn't there?" one of the men remarked. "Sitting just in front of us? But he's nothing to do with us."

And they walked back to the bus, straight past the man who had collapsed, without giving him so much as a glance. To me, they were all Japanese, but he was a tourist from Japan, and they were Americans; he was, in their eyes, no concern of theirs.

MISSOURI AND KANSAS

I sat up in bed in St. Louis, sorting out my maps. The heat-wave had risen to a peak, and even with the air-conditioning turned up to maximum my room was suffocatingly hot.

I had the television on, for company, but as I wanted to concentrate on my route-planning I had turned the sound down to zero. On the silent, brightly-coloured screen vestal virgins danced amateurishly round a make-believe altar; I thought I must have tuned into some re-run of an epic of ancient Rome, but then, moments later, an earnest preacher appeared on the screen. Eyes blazing with sincerity, mouth contorted in what was—to me—a silent exhortation, he had his say and was quickly replaced by a very young girl singing what must—judging by the way she was casting her eyes up to heaven—have been a hymn. I was just thinking how innocent she looked when, peering more closely at the screen, I noticed that her childish face was covered with a thick layer of make-up, as carefully applied as the enamel on a Fabergé egg.

Religion succeeded religion on the screen—parsons, priests and rabbis came, said their piece, and vanished again, separated by angelic choirs and shots of formally-arranged flowers. Outside my bedroom door, an automatic ice-making machine coughed and crashed as it spat cube after cube into a zinc basin; here—as in most American hotels—ice was free.

"I always love to begin a journey on a Sunday," Jonathan

Swift wrote, "because I shall have the prayers of the church, to preserve all that travel by land." After what I had been thinking about those religious broadcasts I doubted if any church would be praying for me, but at least, by starting on a Sunday, I would have the benefit of comparatively truck-free roads. I stuffed my clothes, which I had washed the night before, into my rucksack, wheeled Daisy out under the disapproving stare of the hall porter, and set off westwards.

American suburbs had always seemed vaguely strange to me, but it was not until I was leaving St. Louis that I realised why this was—the houses had no gardens. Around them—where in England there would have been flower-beds and vegetable-patches—was only turf, sometimes edged with low picket fences but more often left completely open to the street. In spite of the large cars parked in the driveways, the fresh paintwork, and the elegant patio furniture, the absence of flowers and vegetables made the surroundings of the houses look rather forlorn.

After the suburbs ended the countryside at first was rolling, with trees and hedges dividing large fields, but about the second day out of St. Louis it flattened, and suddenly the highest things were water-towers and electricity pylons. It seemed a long, long way across Missouri. It was, in fact, a long, long way. I kept myself going by thinking of all the American place-names that had been put into the titles of songs—"Missouri Waltz," "My Old Kentucky Home," "On the Banks of the Wabash," "Meet me in St. Louis," "On the Atcheson Topeka and the Santa Fé," "California, Here I Come." By the time I reached the middle of Missouri I must have tried to sing about fifty different songs.

It was very nice to get to Kansas City—especially so because I reached it on a bath night. I had fallen into a sort of routine—four or five nights sleeping out, then a night in a motel, to bath and wash my hair and clothes. Never again would I laugh at tourists who judged where they were by what day of the week it was, for I myself had started to remember towns by the comfort of their bathrooms. The one in St. Louis had been a real pig—the basin plug missing and the bath run-away choked with hairs

—but this Kansas City one was a honey. I splashed happily in about twenty gallons of hot water, and then—feeling, as usual, exhilaratingly hungry—went downstairs in search of food.

I gave the dining-room door a push; it didn't move, so I pushed harder.

"Not open yet," said a male voice behind me. I turned and saw a man slouched in one of the lounge armchairs. "But the bar is. Care to join me while we wait?" He stood up, revealing himself as quite extraordinarily tall.

"That's very kind of you, but I think I'll just go for a little walk."

"Watch out—it's an awful large city to take a little walk in."

It was still light outside, and there were quite a lot of people strolling about in an unhurried sort of way. But although unhurried, they all seemed to be going somewhere, and what's more, going there with somebody else. Suddenly, I felt a twinge of loneliness; I had never experienced this before, perhaps because I'd been travelling so hard that I simply hadn't had time for introspection.

I stepped into a telephone kiosk, with the idea of telephoning home—I did this about once a week, to reassure myself that everyone was all right. But then I remembered that, time-wise, I was about eight hours behind England; it would be the middle of their night—was I justified in waking them up, just because I was feeling blue?

While I considered the problem, I read a small card that was pinned to the wall of the kiosk.

"Lonely?" it said. "Got a problem? We're here to help. Call AA." And it gave a telephone number.

Acting on impulse, I found the necessary coins—and dialled.

"Alcoholics Anonymous," said a bright voice. "My name is Mary and I'm an alcoholic. Can I help you?"

"Well, I'm here on my own, and. . . ."

"Come along and join us, honey. We're having a meeting tonight. Where are you? Don't ring off."

I think it may have been a church hall. I'm not sure. Anyway, it was pretty bleak and depressing. But the moment I walked in I had the sensation of being surrounded with concern.

"I don't think we've seen you here before, have we, dear? Do you find you're having a drink problem?"

I felt a terrible fraud. All that kindness, and I was taking it under false pretences.

"No, I don't think I have. Not yet, anyway. Not so far as I know, that is. It's just that I was feeling a bit lonely. . . ."

"Very wise to come along. Best thing you could have done. That's when it so often starts—folks on their own. But you're not alone any more, dear. Come on over and meet some friends."

Coffee was being handed out by a girl of film-star loveliness—surely she couldn't be an alcoholic, not with all that beauty going for her? But when the coffee was finished and we were sitting on hard little chairs, she was the first to get up and talk to the meeting.

She gave her name, and added, "I'm an alcoholic." And then she spoke, without a trace of embarrassment, about the problems that she had had, and how her life had changed since she'd stopped drinking. More speakers followed, each painting a glowing picture of life without alcohol; they all started their speeches by stating "I am an alcoholic," and after the speeches there was more coffee, and a collecting box was circulated to cover expenses. Someone drove me back to my hotel, saying cheerily, "See you next week?" Grateful for the way my loneliness had been banished, I hadn't the face to confess that by the following week I hoped to be hundreds of miles away.

Still hungry, I went into the hotel bar and ordered a toasted sandwich and, because I was feeling rather exhausted, a large drink. The drink arrived first. It was a double scotch on the rocks and I was sitting admiring it, thinking how nice the amber liquid looked swirling round the transparent lumps of ice, when the tall man came in.

"Hello there! I was looking for you, to see if you'd have cared to join me for dinner. Wherever did you vanish to?"

"Oh . . . . I went to a meeting of Alcoholics Anonymous."

His eyes dropped to the glass on the table in front of me.

The next day promised to bring the start of the most gruelling part of my trip—the vast plain of Kansas. But first I had to get out of the city. Mile after mile of shops, factories, petrol stations, advertisement boardings—Griff's Burger Bar, The Church of the First Assembly of God, The Magic Kiss Car Wash, U-Bring-It (bring what, I wondered?), Exotic Tool Welding Corp., To rent—Loveseats, Glass Doctors—We Mend Your Panes, Active Storage Co., Chili Dogs, Bali Health Spa, Slab Bacon 89c. And everywhere cars, cars, cars. On my tiny bicycle, I began to feel as if I was an amoeba being flushed down a gigantic drain.

I crossed the Missouri. And then crossed it again. And again. Behind me the city faded into the heat haze, seeming—like so many American cities—to gain with distance a magic which lower-built European towns only rarely achieve. London, for all the history that lies within it, does not tempt one to look back; not so St. Louis, or Kansas City, whose sky-scrapers, seen from afar, endow the cities from which they spring with a hazy, Camelot-like beauty.

Eventually even the sky-scrapers vanished. The road, flanked with fields and copses planted with oaks and poplars and small, pretty trees with pink buds, opened out after about 30 miles into rolling pastures, where cream-coloured Charolais browsed in tree-edged fields. Sphere-shaped water-towers loomed above the trees like tethered hot-air balloons. A huge silo, gleaming in the sunshine, pointed skywards with all the aggression of a space-missile. I had reached Abilene, the birthplace of President Eisenhower.

Only a hundred years before, when the railway line was creeping westwards to join up with the one that was coming east, Abilene was one of the roughest cowboy towns in America, standing at the northernmost point of the Chisholm Trail, up which cattle were driven from the grasslands of Texas, to be shipped at Abilene to the meat-hungry markets of the east.

"Wild Bill" Hickok was one of its early marshals, ruling with a six-shooter as many as 5,000 cowboys, paid off in a single night and raising hell in the saloons, gambling joints and brothels. Now the town seemed to have forgotten this part of its history, concentrating single-mindedly on its presidential son; his name was written up everywhere I looked.

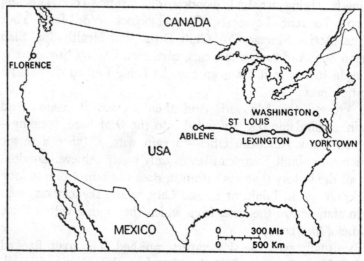

ABILENE, KANSAS

I don't know exactly how long it took me to cross the vast plain that came after Abilene. It seemed to stretch for ever, and ever, and ever. Ten-mile straight stretches of road would be succeeded, after only the slightest of bends, by straight stretches even longer. Oil derricks, each like a huge praying mantis, nodded amid the vivid green of the sprouting corn. Cars and trucks flashed past in both directions, zap, zap, zap; nobody drew up, nobody waved.

There were no village stores, and no way to pick up water between the widely-separated towns that squatted, like untidy parking-lots, beside their water-towers and silos. Camping, too, presented unexpected problems, for the farms were set a long way off the road, and the few signs that indicated camp-sites made no mention of how many miles down side-roads these sites were.

I would pause by a sign pointing down a side-road, straining my eyes to see if I could spot any clue—a tree, perhaps, or a slight bump in the ground—to show where the camp-site might be. But there would be nothing visible at all, and there seemed little point in bicycling perhaps five miles out of my way to look for a camp-site that would almost certainly—if I ever found it— be closed. Once, I bicycled hopefully up to a sign, only to find that it read PRAIRIE DOG TOWN—COME AND VISIT OUR FIVE-LEGGED COW; along the track down which it pointed I could see absolutely nothing except, on the far horizon, a single stunted tree.

There was nothing for it but to camp alongside the road. I didn't want to go too far away from the road and yet I was somehow scared of being too near, so I would compromise by pitching my tent about 50 yards clear of the tarmac, in scrub that would completely hide it. Feeling rather like a hare in a concealed form I would lie looking up at planes criss-crossing the cirrus heights above me; by the next day they would be in Hawaii . . . Hong Kong . . . Hamburg. And where would I be? Still creeping across that endless plain. When I woke in the night, I could hear the cars and trucks still beating their way down the road—zap, zap, zap, zap, zap.

After two—or was it three?—nights by the road, with only the water that I carried in my water-bottle for both drinking and washing, I was so grubby that I decided to spend a night in a motel. As bad luck would have it, I picked a town that was a staging-post for long-distance buses, and arrived just as two buses—coming from opposite directions—converged on the town's only café. I found myself in a queue of about a hundred people, filing past a counter into which were sunk containers filled with seething messes of chili con carne and potatoes, and one labelled—optimistically—Mixed Spring Vegetables. I leant over the counter and caught the eye of a waitress. She was wear-

ing a scarlet Crimplene trouser-suit, and her hair was the colour
of a marmalade cat.

"May I have a plate, please?"

"You've got one, honey."

I looked down at what I had thought was a tray, that I'd
picked up at the start of the line. There were some indentations
in its plastic surface, but the problem was—which indentation
was meant for which type of food? I hesitated, and was instantly
swept past the first—hot—food section by the relentless pressure
of the queue.

The next section was Salads and Desserts. Surely they
couldn't really be charging all that money for two bleached let-
tuce leaves topped with half a tinned peach and a scoop of cottage cheese? And pecan pie—what on earth was pecan pie? In
desperation, feeling the queue treading porpoise-like on my tail,
I grabbed a sort of plastic fig leaf on which was sealed, as if for
all eternity, a piece of plastic cheese, two plastic biscuits, and a
square of plastic butter. Oh good—when one got the outer layer
of plastic off, it was possible to eat what was under it—that is, if
one had remembered to grab a knife as one passed the cash-
register. Which I hadn't, of course—I had to go back.

Another waitress, wearing mauve sandals and a pink mini-
skirt, was going round filling people's coffee-cups from a vacuum
jug; I waited hopefully for ten minutes and then an old hobo,
who'd been there before the buses arrived and would presumably still be there after they left, took pity on me and told me
that though the waitress would fill up a cup, it wasn't any part
of her duties to supply the initial cup—one had to get this by
standing in another queue and holding a cup under the beak of
a fierce, eagle-like machine called Kano, The Koffee King. Kano
had a lot of buttons which one had to press after one had fed
him with a suitably tasty coin—the buttons said COFFEE,
CHOCOLATE, BLACK, WHITE, WITH, WITHOUT, and
REJECT. I hadn't realised that I should put the cup under his
beak before I pressed any of the buttons, and about half my
coffee went into my shoe.

It was quite peaceful in the café after the buses had left, though it would have been even more so if one of the waitresses hadn't put what looked like an entire evening's tips into the juke-box, which immediately started to moan about the miseries of unrequited love. I began to think longingly of bed.

"Please, is there anywhere here that I could stay?"

The marmalade-cat waitress looked at me with an expression of absolute, complete and total boredom.

"Stay here if you want—we don't close till after the bus from Denver goes by."

"I mean stay the night. A room."

"Well—I don't rightly know. Most folks, they go straight through—sleep on the bus. There's the Fringed Surrey, down the road, but that's usually all full up by evening. Families driving—wanting to get kids to bed early. You could try, though."

I couldn't miss the Fringed Surrey, not only because it had a neon-outlined sign in the shape of a Victorian hansom cab, but also because the side-road, on which the town stood, appeared to end only about 20 yards beyond it. It consisted of about twelve shabby little cabins; over the door of the first one hung a flashing sign, saying VACANCIES, and a second sign, not flashing, saying RECEPTION. The door was locked, but through the glass I could see a man and a woman in a back room, watching television. I rang the bell. Nothing happened. I rang again, harder; this time I could actually hear the bell pealing inside the cabin. Still no reaction. In desperation, I hammered on the glass. The woman got up, took off a safety chain, and opened the door.

"No need to make that racket. You could've rung."

"I did."

"Can't have, or I'd've heard it."

No point in arguing, I thought. "I'd like a room, please. For one night."

"Nup. No vacancy."

I began to feel my hackles rising. "Then why is that sign on—VACANCY?"

"One of the kids must've switched it on. Or mebbe my husband forgot to switch it off." She turned and shouted into the room behind her, "We ain't got no vacancy, have we?"

The man got up and sauntered through, carrying an open beer can. His eyes were blood-shot and his chin carried several days' growth of beard. "Sure, we've got a vacancy. Number seventeen. Checked out late."

The woman looked at him with an expression of mixed exasperation and hatred.

"So now you tell me. And who's going to make the room up, at this hour?" The lines that ran from her nostrils to the corners of her mouth might have been caused by habitual bad temper, but they might equally well have been the result of exhaustion.

Number seventeen was—of all things—underground, but I didn't discover this until, finding its dampness oppressive, I drew back the curtains from what I thought was a window and found myself facing a blank wall. The bath water hiccoughed reluctantly from the taps, tepid and strangely streaked with foam. Even the television—that staple of American motels—was out of order; through what seemed to be a snowstorm localised behind the screen I watched disinterestedly as policemen shot gangsters, gangsters shot policemen and, finally, someone unrolled a map of America and explained what the weather was likely to be the next day. As the meteorologist moved his baton from state to state I realised with a sort of panic that I didn't know where I was. I switched off the set and lay in the dark, mentally trying to orientate myself on an imaginary map. Not knowing where I was was curiously alarming, like looking in a mirror and not seeing a reflection gazing back.

The next morning, failing to find anywhere else to eat, I went back to the bus café for breakfast. The clock over the counter had only just touched seven-thirty, but already the juke-box was yowling; there was a slotted box beside every table, into which one could put coins to make it work, and it never stopped for more than a few moments without a customer urging it on with yet another coin.

The food in the serving-troughs had been changed to a yellowish substance labelled SCRAMBLED EGGS and another—brownish—marked PAN-FRIED IDAHO POTATOES. The waitress in the mauve sandals was already circulating with the coffee-jug, while the marmalade-cat one stood behind the serving-counter, tipping reddish-yellow granules into a glass urn; she studied the level of the granules in the urn, topped it up from a jug of water, gave the resultant mixture a brisk, professional stir, and set in front of it a plastic notice reading FRESHLY SQUEEZED ORANGE JUICE.

A man in working overalls sat in one of the booths, gloomily ploughing his way through three assorted helpings of cereal; finishing the Sugar Puffs, he placed—on top of the empty bowl—a second bowl containing Coco Crispies and—the Coco Crispies demolished—topped the pile with a third bowl holding Bran Buds. Throughout the operation his jaws ground relentlessly from side to side, like those of a ruminating ox. Beside the window sat a group of men wearing scarlet hunting caps; their guns were leant against their chairs, as if they half expected that an enemy might suddenly appear in the street.

The old hobo sat slouched in a corner, gazing disconsolately at a dingy ashtray; I persuaded Kano to disgorge two cups of watery brown liquid and carried them over. I pushed one cup tentatively towards him.

"Care to join me?"

"Couldn't impose on you, lady."

"Nonsense—what can I do with two cups?"

I studied him as he drank. His eyes—set under brows as shaggy as the eaves of a thatched cottage—were red-rimmed and curiously fierce-looking, and the fingers with which he steadied the coffee cup were so caked with grime that they resembled the blackened ends of over-ripe bananas. He seemed to be wearing two coats, both of them so ragged that it was hard to make out where one ended and the other began.

After a minute he put down his cup, coughed hoarsely, and came out with the standard question.

"Where'you from?"

It was as if each word had to choose between fighting its way over the stumps of his decaying teeth or falling out through the gaps where his teeth were missing, and if I hadn't heard that particular question dozens of times before I don't think I'd have grasped what he was saying.

"England."

"W'ch part?"

It never crossed my mind that he would have visited England, so I gave my standard answer.

"Near London."

"North or south?"

"West, actually. About 60 miles."

"Indeedy. Used to know it quite well, round there. Little town called . . . let me see . . . Newburg?"

"Newbury?"

"That was it. Near the airfield." His voice seemed to lose its mumbling slur, revealing traces of a lost decisiveness.

"But I live very near it—the airfield. Whatever took you there?"

"Navigator." He mentioned a type of plane, but the name meant nothing to me. "In the war. But you wouldn't remember," he added, with an unexpected touch of gallantry.

"Of course I remember."

We sat opposite each other in that sleazy café, somewhere in the middle of I didn't know where, and it looked as if neither of us knew what to say next. I don't know what he was thinking, but I know what I was—I was remembering the Americans whom I had danced with at a Forces Club, when I was still a girl in my teens. Self-confident airmen, smart and handsome in their uniforms, who would be at the club one week and the next week might have vanished, perhaps to another posting, perhaps —who knows? Could we have danced together once, I wondered, all that time ago, when the world was young? But that was in another country . . . and if we had, I don't think either of us could have borne to recall it. As I left the café, I turned to give him a farewell wave, but he was looking in the other direction, towards the coffee-carrying waitress in the mauve sandals.

Recalling my girlhood made me think back still further—to my school-days—and as I bicycled out of the town I suddenly remembered that if one laid one's school ruler up the almost vertical east coast of Mexico, and, using it as a guide, drew a line straight up through the United States, then all the area on the right-hand side of the line would—or so my geography mistress had said—have vegetation similar to England, while immediately to the left of the line it would be like that of the southern Sahara—the part that lies between the sand dunes of romantic films and the grasslands that fringe the northern limits of the equatorial Congo basin. I must, I thought, be just about crossing that imaginary ruler-line, and the idea was rather exciting.

But as I bicycled westwards, my enthusiasm was blighted by the blank greyness that seemed to be falling over the plain. It was neither a mist nor an unusually early dusk, though it seemed to have something of the qualities of both; it evened out distances, flattening the landscape until I felt that instead of travelling forward I was struggling to climb the vertical two-dimensional perspective of a stage backcloth.

And then the wind started. At first it was hardly more than a gentle breeze—a series of playful puffs that might have been initiated by one of those cherubs that pose, all dimples and curls, in the corners of medieval maps. It tweaked the grass at the edge of the road, and bent the green tips of the sprouting corn in nearby fields into swirling patterns as delicate as watered silk.

But then it strengthened. Brightly-coloured discarded cigarette packets bowled down the road like somersaulting circus clowns. My hat flew backwards off my head and hung, trapped by its elastic loop, down the back of my shirt. Telegraph wires, strung along the side of the road on lonely poles, started to hum, as if bearing warnings of some mysterious impending disaster. Brought up on the Wizard of Oz, I had been subcon-

sciously prepared, when crossing Kansas, to be whisked up
in a twisting tornado and deposited in a land of Munchkins,
but I certainly wasn't prepared for the reality—the stinging,
suffocating dust-storm that suddenly enveloped me.

It was coming at me head-on, driving into my eyes, my ears
and my mouth. I put on my sun-glasses, but this only made mat-
ters worse, because not only did the sand still get into my eyes
but the combination of the dark lenses and the gloom of the
storm made it almost impossible to see where I was going. Next
I fumbled in my rucksack, searching for my headscarf to tie over
my mouth; I found it, but before I could tie it on the wind
snatched it from my fingers and swept it a hundred yards down
the road; I went back, but by the time I reached it, it was half
buried under a swirl of dust as neat as the top of a meringue.

Soon, the wind got so strong that I could no longer bicycle
against it; I got off and walked, pushing Daisy. Cars went past,
headlights blazing; after a while I made some feeble attempts to
hitch a ride, but nobody stopped—either they didn't see me or,
with my scarf tied over my nose, I looked too sinister for safety.

I thought of putting up my tent and bivouacing in it till the
storm was over, but I had no idea of whether the fury would last
a few hours or a few days, and as I had very little water with me
I thought I'd better struggle on. By now the sand was gritting
between my teeth, forming scratchy deposits in the crevasses of
my gums, like the debris of drilled-out amalgam filling.

But then, just when I was wondering if I was going to col-
lapse, I walked slap into a petrol station. There was nobody at
the pumps, but twenty yards behind them a sign flashed.
SCANDINAVIAN SMOREBROD, it proclaimed, SCAN-
DINAVIAN SMOREBROD, ALL YOU CAN EAT FOR $3.
I leant Daisy against a Coke machine, and went in.

I think I half expected to find a bunch of stranded des-
perados, ready to fight each other for even a sip of water. What
in fact I saw was a group of very normal-looking travellers, eating at a white-clothed table. Behind them ran a long, brightly-lit

serving counter set out with dishes of pickled herrings, hard boiled eggs, strips of cheese, potatoes in mayonnaise, chili beans, cubed ham, sliced beetroot, tossed green salad and cold roast beef.

As I lurched in at the door, the heads of all the diners turned towards me, like those of Centre Court spectators following the flight of a tennis ball.

"Hello!" I squeaked. The sand seemed to have maimed my vocal cords, making normal speech impossible.

Nobody answered. They just turned their heads away and resumed eating. I walked unsteadily past them and went into the lavatory, which was labelled—predictably—Rest Room, and peered into a looking-glass; my eyes had dirt goggles round them and the rest of me looked as if I'd climbed out of the dust bag of a Hoover. No wonder those well-scrubbed diners hadn't exactly rolled out the welcome mat.

I dunked a disgracefully extravagant number of paper towels into the basin and did an emergency repair job; the diners glanced up in a faintly hostile way when I reappeared, but nobody actually told me to go away, so I sat down. A waitress lounged up, order-pad in hand.

"May I have a glass of beer, please?"

"Don't serve beer here. You can get it at the gas station."

No beer with smorebrod? Beer with petrol? How confusing.

"A glass of water, then. And a hamburger, please."

"Eat or take?"

I wasn't quite sure what she meant. Obviously, if I was asking for it, I must want to eat it, and if I was going to eat it surely I had to take it? I hesitated, and the waitress sighed impatiently.

"D'you want to eat it here, or take it with you on the bus?"

So that was why all these people were eating in what seemed to be outer space—they must be bus passengers, and this must be a rest halt. Suddenly I had an idea.

"Could you just have it cooked for me, and I'll let you know? And please, which is the driver of the bus?"

I just had time to buy a large can of beer, and fold up Daisy. Then, clutching the hot, juicy hamburger in one still dusty-nailed hand, I was off down the road to Denver, Colorado. Only this time I was sitting in the front seat of a Greyhound bus.

KANSAS AND COLORADO

At that precise moment, I could think of absolutely no greater happiness than to be exactly where I was, bowling effortlessly over the plain in the front seat of a Greyhound bus. Every mile that the bus covered was to me a supreme luxury, simply because I wasn't having to cover it under my own steam; going uphill was an absolutely exquisite pleasure, for did I not know— only too well—how much effort it took to pedal Daisy up even a modest rise? And the peak of happiness, after so much thirst, was to be travelling with my hand tightly wrapped round an open can of ice-cold beer; my hand had to be tightly wrapped round it, for I was sitting directly under a notice saying THE DRINKING OF ALCOHOLIC BEVERAGES IS FORBIDDEN ON THIS BUS.

Twenty-five miles saw us clear of the dust-storm; fifty more, and we were actually in rain. The road stretched ahead, a gleaming silver ribbon. I was warm and comfortable, and I hadn't a care in the world. Unless one could count as a care the fact that I hadn't the faintest idea where I was going to sleep that night— but then, having not known that on any day since I left home, this was hardly likely to worry me.

I leant forward and, in the curved mirror above the driver's head, studied the passengers sitting behind me. Somebody had told me that every Greyhound carried at least one grandmother, crossing the continent to inspect a new grandchild; and yes, there was the grandmother for this bus, sitting two rows back. Grey-haired, benign, she was knitting a Tiny Garment. Grandmothers of the World, Unite, I thought, moving to sit beside her.

"That's nice. What's it going to be?"

"A jacket—for my latest grandchild." She held up an intricately-patterned oblong, and drew a further length of baby-pink wool from a plastic bag.

"How many grandchildren have you got?"

"This'll be—let me see—sixty-eight."

"*Sixty-eight?*"

"Oh yes. Last time, she just had the one. But the time before, it was four. Her sister, she doesn't usually have more than two or three at once—but then, she's a lot smaller."

I groped for a suitable comment. "It must be very interesting for you, having so many."

"It is—it is indeed. Especially as one never really knows exactly what colour they're going to turn out, no matter how careful one is."

I sat in stunned silence while she did some intricate shaping round what appeared to be a neck-edge. Then she went on, "Would you like to see their photos?"

"I'd really love to." Indeed, I could hardly wait.

She fished in the canvas carry-all that was standing on the floor between us and pulled out a booklet entitled *Cherish Your Colon.*

"Oh bother, that's not it." She fished again, and this time producing one of those wallets that hold plastic display envelopes. She flicked it open, exhibiting about twenty photos of Pekingese, each one sporting a little knitted jacket.

"Aren't they darlings? I bred their mothers, every one of them. They're all over the States now—it takes me best part of two months out of the year, just visiting them. Costs the earth in fares. But it's worth it, every cent." She kissed a page, and I saw tears of emotion in her eyes.

"Say, where'you from?" queried a man who had been sitting

in the seat behind us. He had stood up and leaned forward, so that when I turned to answer him the button on the top of my hat hit his teeth with the clicking sound of a billiard-cue striking a ball.

"So sorry. . . ."

"Don't mention it. My fault entirely. Hope you don't mind my talking to you."

"Not a bit. England."

The man turned round so that his back was towards me—a difficult manoeuvre, as there was very little space between the rows of seats.

"Say—Lureen!" he yelled.

At the back of the bus, a girl with over-bleached hair stirred irritably, peering over the collar of the mackintosh under which she had been dozing.

"What was the name of that town in England that your sister-in-law came from, Lur?"

The girl appeared to search her mind. Then, "Edinburgh," she yelled back, pulling the mackintosh up over her face, so that all that could be seen of her was her tufty hair, sticking up from the transparent plastic like a washing-up brush upended in a jar.

"Yea, that was it, Edinburgh," said the man with satisfaction, turning back to me. "Heard of it?" Both he and the girl pronounced it to rhyme with iceberg.

"Oh yes. It's a beautiful city."

"Is that so? She sure was a beautiful girl, too. We were quite upset when she took off."

"What happened? I mean—don't tell me if you'd rather not."

"Oh, it's no secret. Lur's brother, he was in the navy; nothing much to look at—I guess she only married him to get over here. Must be pretty grim in England, eh? All that fog. Anyway, after he got his discharge, he got a job in a gas station. Out in the desert. Damn all for her to do, recreationwise, so she used to help out—take the cash and so on. Well, she cleared off with some guy in a Cadillac. Old enough to be her father. Only stopped for some gas, and pow! darned if he didn't take her along with his change."

I admired some more pictures of Pekes, then I moved back into my own seat, and snoozed; the road raced wetly beneath the bus, like a treadmill accelerated to manic speed. After about an hour I became conscious of somebody coughing—not a sick cough, but the discreet throat-clearing of someone who is anxious to attract attention. I opened my eyes.

"Ah! You're awake. I guessed you were," said a bald-headed man who had, while I dozed, taken the seat next to mine. "May I introduce myself? The Reverend. . . ."

I didn't catch his name—or rather, I heard it, but it slipped immediately from my mind. I responded with my own name, and in the confines of adjoining seats we shook hands awkwardly, like two acquaintances coincidentally crippled in their right arms.

"Travelling alone?"

"Yes."

"Ah! I thought so—I can always tell."

"I quite like travelling alone, actually."

"Ah! In the voyage of life we are all lonely travellers, till we reach out and take the hand of Jesus."

Speak for yourself, I thought irritably, overcome with the desire to go back to sleep. "Frankly, I've got some good friends here on earth, too. I can't honestly say I'm lonely."

"Ah! But you delude yourself, my child. You are lonely without being aware of your loneliness. You will never know true comradeship until you admit the misery of earthly loneliness, and accept with humility the sacred friendship of the Lord."

"I really do appreciate your bothering about me, but I'm awfully tired. I think perhaps I might catch a little more sleep."

"Sleep? Sleep? I have here a little pamphlet. . . ." and he produced, apparently from thin air, a stapled wad of foolscap. "A little pamphlet. Ah. To read this will give you more solace than sleep. To hark to the words of our Saviour will refresh more than just your weary limbs. To. . . ."

"I'm sorry," I interrupted desperately. "Reading in buses makes me feel sick."

"Then—ah—I will read to you. Close your eyes, and listen to the words of comfort, as set down by our brother. . . ."

I shut my eyes and rested my head against the window, but as this took my ear further away he instantly compensated by leaning over my seat, and in a monotone—interspersed with staccato Ahs!—began to read me a tract so incomprehensible, so crammed with anomalies and nonsequiturs, that I found myself positively compelled to give up any attempt at understanding. Allowing the drone of his voice to wash over me like a river, I tried to drift into sleep, but just as I thought I was dropping off I felt the pressure of a hand on my knee. I thought the Reverend was simply emphasising a point, but then I felt the hand move an inch more, and then another. I opened one eye and glanced downwards.

Sure enough, under cover of the tract, a hand like an emaciated spider was crawling cautiously up my leg. The Reverend, meanwhile, was continuing to read as if totally unconscious of what his hand was doing.

"Excuse me," I said, getting up and heading for the Rest Room at the back of the bus. How much of a long bus-ride, I wondered, could one spend standing in a compartment only a yard square, with a greasy hand-basin on one side and a chemical WC on the other?

I watched with relief the Reverend getting off at a town called, of all things, Angelus. When I went back to my seat I found some more roneod tracts arranged on it; they were headed, I'm glad to say, with the name of an organisation I'd never heard of. Perhaps the Reverend was the only member.

I dozed again, and when I next awoke we were passing over rough scrub country, liberally dusted with snow. Snow? In late May? And over there—on the tops of some low hills that were just appearing over the horizon—there was even more snow. I shook myself awake, and looked again; those were no low hills—

they were the peaks of the Rocky Mountains, seen from very far away.

Then, as the towers of Denver rose above the intervening country, the Rockies seemed to recede, to vanish into the greyish mist that lay below the blaze of the setting sun. But I couldn't fool myself that they weren't there, and when the bus arrived in Denver I checked into a first-class hotel and got myself a spacious room on the twentieth floor; I felt I needed some luxury before I tackled those Rockies.

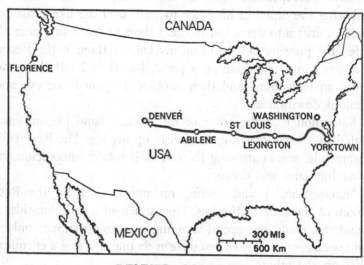

DENVER, COLORADO

The room was expensive, but my cash was holding out better than I had expected. I'd started off with a money-clip of dollars, a folder of traveller's cheques, and an internationally-recognised credit card, and as I'd never had to pay for a camp-site and my food was usually very simple I was living, if anything, more cheaply than I would have done had I stayed at home. The whole trip, I calculated, would cost very little more than a conventional package-tour holiday, so I didn't feel too guilty on the few occasions that I really spoilt myself.

The television set in my penthouse room had the biggest screen I had ever seen; I switched it on as soon as I woke up the next morning hoping for a weather forecast, but every station seemed to be showing cartoons. Talking ducks followed smart mice, bears in ranger hats succeeded ingenious alley-cats, mini-skirted cave-girls came after ghost hunting hounds. When a weather map finally appeared on the screen, I realised that once again I wasn't really quite sure where I was. I knew I was in Denver, Colorado—but where exactly was Denver on that cloud-swirled satellite chart? I got out my map.

There was Denver—about 105 degrees west and nearly 40 degrees north; in other words, due north of a vast expanse of empty Pacific and roughly on a level with Madrid and Peking. Encouragingly, it also seemed to be considerably nearer the Pacific than the Atlantic. But against this, the bit of the map that I'd already crossed was mostly coloured green, while the part that still lay ahead was almost entirely beige and brown, with sinister streaks of white. There was no shutting my eyes to what those colours meant—until I actually reached the Pacific, I would seldom be bicycling at less than 1,000 feet, and most of the time I would be very much higher.

The previous evening, I had left Daisy in a locker at the bus station feeling—as I dismantled her—considerable gratitude towards the man who had invented her; I would never have been able to jump so easily on a bus if I had had a normal bike (bus companies, like the airlines, demand that normal bikes be packed in cumbersome crates) and I wouldn't have been able to store even the average folding bike in a locker. But Daisy broke down easily into a tidy jungle of tubes and wires that, resting on the floor, barely reached my finger-tips, and could be tucked away in any place that would take a suitcase. I set off for the bus station to rescue her.

It was a glorious morning, the bright, crisp air reminding me of early spring in Switzerland, an impression heightened by the snow-crowned Rockies lying along the horizon. As I walked through the clean, wide streets of Denver I was suddenly filled

with a great sense of elation—I had crossed more than half of
America. The coastal plain of the east, the Appalachians, and
the vast central plain now lay behind me, and all that remained
ahead were the Rockies, the high plateau beyond the Rockies,
and the area of the western coast. I hurried happily along among
the commuters and schoolchildren, revelling in the bright sunshine.

Inside the bus station the sunlight was replaced by the glare
of fluorescent strips, and the cheerful noises of the streets by a
rasping Tannoy voice announcing the departure of buses to
what seemed to be all points of the compass—west to San Francisco, east to Chicago, south to Santa Fé, north to Cheyenne.
Queues formed in front of the glass doors that led out to the
buses, were released and, like water flowing from tap to drain,
were swallowed up by the waiting vehicles. Filled buses pulled
out on to the highway, accelerated out of sight, and were replaced immediately by others.

Weary-looking transit passengers eased themselves down the
steps of arriving buses, and headed, dazed, towards the Rest
Rooms. Would-be travellers lined up at the ticket-counters,
their features appearing flattened by the fluorescent lighting;
others slouched apathetically on plastic seats, leafing uninterest-
edly through the pages of comics. Overweight children gnawing
on candy bars sat slumped in front of tiny individual TV sets,
stirring only to demand more money to feed into the slots of the
machines. Harassed-looking women followed by demanding
toddlers pushed clattering trays down the counter of the cafeteria, garnering tall glasses filled with what appeared to be
whipped-up shaving soap, and spotty youths sucked like un-
weaned calves at the necks of upturned Coke bottles.

The lockers—in one of which I had imprisoned Daisy—were
banked against the walls, grey with a colour-code on the locks. I
pulled the key of mine from my pocket; it had a red top. There
seemed to be hundreds of lockers in the bus station—yellow-
code, blue-code, white-code; the red-code ones were among the
vending machines (sandwiches, fruit, chocolate bars and frank-

furters, each locked behind a little glass door awaiting, like Cinderella dreaming of a prince's kiss, the liberating touch of a 25-cent piece). As I was putting my key into what I hoped was the right lock, it struck me that the lockers looked just like the rows of refrigerated boxes into which corpses are put in morgues. Hastily, I opened the small metal door—thank goodness, it really was Daisy inside, not a body. I carried her to the door, and started to reassemble her.

By now I had had quite a bit of practice in unfolding Daisy's arms and legs and transforming her from what might have been mistaken for a heap of junk into a fully-operative bicycle. I could do the job in three minutes flat, but during those minutes I hardly ever failed to collect an audience.

As soon as I took her out of her canvas bag I would notice passers-by beginning to slow up; when I straightened the central hinge—revealing that she was some sort of machine—people would begin to gather around. Then the handlebars would pivot, rising from their folded position alongside the front wheel into their normal riding angle, and the questions would start.

"Say, is that a bicycle you've got there?"

"Yes indeed."

"No kidding?"

By this time I would have slipped the seat tube into its socket, and would be crawling around tightening various bolts. I never managed to work out the right answer to "No kidding?" so I would just go on working and wait for the next question, which was usually—

"Where'you from?"

"England."

More crawling, checking and tightening.

"You don't say."

One of the nice things about travelling on a bicycle is that one can break off such obviously unproductive conversations without giving offence. Shutting a car door has a certain abruptness, an air of deliberately excluding the person who is left standing—perhaps with something still to say—on the side of the road. But with a bicycle one can pedal a yard or two, make some trifling (and probably unnecessary) adjustment to a wire or clip, cruise around for a moment and then, with a smile and a wave, simply set off.

I had to be fairly decisive about getting away, or I would have spent too many hours repeating—to fresh groups of spectators—exactly what I was up to. It was flattering that people were interested, but I simply had to get on with the trip.

Now I made some little circles among the parked cars near the Denver bus station, to show the watchers that Daisy really worked, and then, spotting a gap in the traffic, headed off towards the Rockies.

This was one morning when I really didn't need a map, for there wasn't a ghost of a chance of mistaking the direction in which I should go. Westwards, on the far side of a flattish stretch of land that looked strangely like a coastal plain, the Rockies rose almost vertically, like gigantic, mythically unclimbable cliffs. They seemed to tower straight up into the clouds and, from that distance, appeared to have no roads or passes. How, oh how, was I ever going to cross them? I kept on pedalling towards them, telling myself that the only thing was to get there—and try.

But as I bicycled along, I began to feel very sick. At first I thought that the extra-special dinner that I'd stood myself the evening before had been too much for my frugal stomach, but then I remembered how high Denver was above sea-level. Mountain sickness, I told myself gloomily.

There was nothing for it but to halt until my blood got used to the altitude, so although it was only lunch-time I put up my tent in the yard of an obliging scrap-merchant and, surrounded by the stacked-up skeletons of abandoned cars, crept fully dressed into my sleeping-bag. It wasn't the most salubrious of camp-sites, but I felt too weak to pedal another yard, and as even the thought of food made my stomach cringe I wasn't at all put out by the fact that all I had with me was my bottle of water and some rather ancient bread.

Feeling too dizzy even to read, I shut my eyes and dozed, and when I awoke, night had fallen. I unzipped the door of my tent and peered out.

The night was calm and still and very cold, the darkness broken only by the searchlight-sweep of the headlamps of distant cars and, high overhead, the winking navigation lights of a passing plane. Silhouetted against the skyline glow of Denver, the piles of wrecked cars around me loomed like giant tidal waves of metal; the wind, snaking through a hundred rusty keyholes and broken exhaust pipes, moaned and hooted with eerie malevolence.

I zipped the door hurriedly shut again and tried to pretend that I was back in my own bed at home.

Suddenly it was morning and, only half awake, I imagined that someone was tapping on my bedroom door. I opened my eyes, unzipped the top of the door, and peered cautiously out—the tapping sound was being made by an elderly man standing about fifty yards away, chopping wood. He was feeding each piece, as he split it, into a little stove made from an old petrol can, on the top of which was standing a blue enamel coffee-pot. Feeling rather like a snake shedding its skin, I wriggled out of my sleeping-bag.

"Hi there!" said the man. "You awake?"

He was wearing one of those jackets with vertical slits for pockets, and as he walked across to where I was sitting—half in and half out of my tent—he slid his hands rapidly in and out of the slits, as if trying to warm them by friction.

"Boss said not to wake you if you was still sleepin'."

"What time is it?"

"Gone seven. Wouldn't be here if it hadn't." He laughed cheerfully, exhibiting broken, tobacco-stained teeth. "Care for a cup of coffee?"

"Thanks—I'd love some."

He glanced around, upended a disintegrating bench seat that must have been torn from one of the wrecks, and, using the side of his sleeve, gave it a careful dust. Ceremoniously, he placed it

—broken springs twanging—outside my tent. We sat companionably sipping the gritty coffee while the early sun, sparkling on such chrome as had not yet been eaten away by rust, turned the piled-up car-bodies into Everests of glinting metal.

It seemed only polite, in return for the coffee, to volunteer some information.

"I'm heading for Oregon."

"By y'self?"

"Yes—with my bicycle." I hadn't felt strong enough to dismantle Daisy the night before, so had not been able to pull her into the tent; she was leaning against the bashed-in door of a derelict Mercedes, looking, in comparison to the monster that was supporting her, even smaller than usual. The man studied her incredulously.

"You mean you're going to ride that thing? Over there?" He pointed towards the mountains, holding his finger almost vertical, as if to emphasise the steepness of the climb.

"Well—yes. I mean, that's what I was planning to do. What do you think?"

"I think you're plumb crazy, that's what I think. More coffee?"

The sun rose higher, warming the back of my neck and outlining, as if with a giant paint-brush loaded with Chinese White, the snowy heights that towered ahead. The old man watched me sceptically as I rolled up my tent and sleeping-bag and fixed them to Daisy.

"Thanks a lot for the coffee. And would you thank the other man for letting me camp here?"

I had been going to say "thank your boss" but it seemed rude to demote him so obviously to the role of employee. He half raised his hand, as if to wave goodbye, then suddenly thrust rough-nailed fingers into the pocket of his trousers, fumbled for a moment, and brought out some creased dollar bills.

"Here—you go get yourself a bus ticket. Don't like to see you travellin' like that."

"No—really, I like bicycling."

"Go on, take it. I can spare it."

I looked at his frayed shirt and the broken laces in his shoes, and felt a great urge to hug him.

"You're very, very kind. But I can't take it. Please. I'm fine, really I am." And I pedalled away as quickly as the bumpy ground of the scrap-yard would allow.

At the gate I paused, and turned to wave. He was still standing there, looking somehow baffled and lonely, the smoke from the oil-can stove rising thinly behind him like an uncoded message from an Indian signal fire.

COLORADO (2)

It just wasn't going to be possible. I knew it. I sat at the foot of the Rockies and gazed hopelessly at the steep iron-grey road that wound upwards, following the course of a river, until it was lost from sight among the towering, threatening crags.

After only a few miles of bicycling, my mountain sickness had come back; I felt dizzy and weak, and in the pit of my stomach a demoralising feeling was lurking, like the dull weight that, as a child, I had experienced on my way to the dentist. There was absolutely no way, I realised, that I could force my shaking legs up that forbidding road; disconsolately, I flopped face-downwards on the grass of a roadside meadow and tried to think what to do next.

Suddenly I heard a sound in the air above me—something half way between the hiss of a taut sail and the rustle of wind-blown leaves. I rolled on to my back and looked up. A vast bird, like Sinbad's roc, was swooping down on me.

"Sorry if I frightened you," apologised the thin young man, panting slightly as he stumbled to a halt. Above and behind him, the multi-coloured triangle of his hang-glider framed him like half-folded wings, giving him the look of a stained-glass saint in a cathedral window. "Thought I'd get clean over you, but I guess I ran out of sky." Deftly, he unbuckled himself and laid the glider on the grass. "Jeese, that was a hairy ride."

Sitting down beside me, he pulled out a packet of cigarettes.

"Care for a smoke?"

I shook my head. "Hairy?"

"Thermals kinda haywire." He turned over on to his back and smoked silently for a few minutes. Then he glanced at Daisy. "Which way you going?"

"I was meaning to cross the pass, but it doesn't look as if I'll make it."

"How so?"

"I think the altitude's got me."

"Could give you a lift part of the way, if you like. My recovery team should be down soon, and we'll be heading back that way."

Half an hour later I was riding up towards the pass in the front seat of an enormous car, Daisy tucked into what I would have called the boot but which the driver referred to as his trunk. The other occupants of the car were talking animatedly in hang-glider language, and behind us, as the car ground up the precipitous inclines, swayed an elongated trailer packed with gliders, their huge triangle-shapes as neatly folded as the wings of sleeping bats.

Somehow, I had always imagined the Rockies to be picturesque tree-clad mountains, decorated in almost equal parts by clear rushing streams, leaping trout, amiable bears, and singing film-stars, and I was completely unprepared for the reality, which was precipitous, bleak, and very forbidding. I hadn't even the slightest urge to do any part of the climb on my own, and when the driver pulled off the road at a point which was obviously not the top of the pass I felt distinctly glum.

Everyone but me piled out of the car and peered—over what seemed to be a terrifying drop—towards the plain behind us. I was selfishly glad when they came back to the car.

"Hey—doesn't look as if we'll fly again till evening. Would you like us to run you right up to the top? Got loads of time on our hands."

The pass was deep in snow, the road winding over it like a dribble of dirty oil. A large notice stood outlined against some miserable-looking fir trees; it announced that the elevation was 11,307 feet and that the pass was a watershed between the Atlantic and the Pacific. I had hoped for a cheery café, of the kind that one finds at the top of Alpine ski-lifts, but as the glider boys reversed their trailer-car and set off down the road we had just climbed I found myself completely alone. There was just the snow, the trees, the lowering sky—and the sinister-looking grey road, snaking away downwards towards the distant Pacific; I rode a few yards down it, and then I got off again. I might as well, I thought, take a photograph, just to remember what the Continental Divide looked like.

Lacking a human companion to decorate the foreground of photographs, I had by now taken literally dozens of snaps of Daisy, posed beside everything from Yorktown's George III cannons to Mississippi paddleboats. Now, on top of the Rockies, I leant her against a post at the side of the road, and stepped back to immortalise her against a panorama of snow and sky.

I fumbled with the little slide-thing that was supposed to adjust the distance on my camera, and peered through the viewfinder. Yes, there was the post—outlined against the sky. But where was Daisy? I took the camera away from my eye and gazed unbelievingly. Daisy had completely vanished. I hastened, slipping on the icy tarmac, back to the post; a flurry of snow in the ravine that lay behind it told me how idiotic I'd been not to test the firmness of the patch of snow on which I had left her—it had given way, and Daisy, with all my gear lashed to her, had fallen about 60 feet down the ravine.

It took three trips down the ravine to get everything up—two for the gear and one for Daisy herself—and on the third ascent I didn't know whether I was crying from exasperation, exhaustion, or just simple pain. The pain was because somewhere on the second descent—which I'd done by sitting on my heels and tobogganing down—the soles had ripped completely off my shoes. They were still attached at the back, but from my insteps forward they just flapped, like the lower jaws of a pair of paranoiac crocodiles. I tried putting my socks on outside my shoes;

this held the soles in their right position until the socks themselves gave out, after which it was simply Every Toe for Itself—and the unlucky ones went straight down on to below-zero rock.

Gibbering with misery, I finally got everything back on to the road, and, tying the soles of my shoes to my insteps with two guy-lines off my tent, started off down the far side of the pass.

At first the road wasn't particularly steep, but then it suddenly turned into an imitation of the Cresta Run. The wheels of the bicycle were going round so fast that the spokes—cutting through the freezing air—made a noise like a swarm of bees. Worse than that, the brake-pads started to melt, giving off a smell like burnt toast.

I slithered to a stop, and stood shivering at the roadside while the brakes cooled; the rims of the wheels, as well as the actual pads, were too hot to touch. In fact, just about the only thing that didn't seem in danger of melting was me—I was not only half-frozen, but also soaking wet; the snow that had collected in the folds of my clothes as I struggled up and down the ravine had melted into an icy mush that had penetrated right through to my skin.

I coasted downhill, stopping every few minutes to allow the wheels to cool, and also to glance anxiously at the sun, which was edging its usual inexorable way towards the savage-looking horizon. I had become, by now, fairly adept at judging the time of day by the angle of the sun, and when it got to about 45 degrees above the western horizon I would usually start looking for a camp-site. But that day, although the sun was already obviously sinking, I didn't dare halt; or, to be more exact, there wasn't much point in halting, because the country was scaringly wild and the temperature equally scaringly low, and I had a horrid conviction that if I camped I would die either of fright or hypothermia, or quite possibly both. I really had to find somewhere warm and dry to sleep, and when I reached a tiny town to the west of the watershed, I booked into the first motel and tottered straight from a hot bath into bed.

When I woke up the next morning a revving and roaring and

spluttering of motor-bicycles was shaking the wooden walls of
my motel, causing the twin tooth-glasses in the bathroom to
judder on their plastic shelf and the wire coat-hangers to
shimmy along the metal rod of the wardrobe. I slipped out of
bed and, pulling on my T-shirt, drew back the curtains; not
more than a couple of yards away from my window a posse of
leather-clad motor-bicyclists was vrmm-vrmming their machines, as if in preparation for a take-off into outer space. Their
helmets, domed like those of astronauts but sharing, because of
their raised visors, a curiously anachronistic kinship with the
headgear of crusading knights, were decorated with the painted
emblems of yet a third culture—the feathers and tomahawks of
American Indians. Suddenly, as if to confuse both time and culture still further, they formed a line astern that might have been
modelled on the battle-order of some Napoleonic sea-fight, and
roared off down the wide street.

In the silence that followed their departure, I began to hear
the small domestic sounds of a town awakening—the whirr of an
electric razor, the clatter of a frying-pan, the slam of a refrigerator door. I pushed the window up and leant out, elbows on
sill.

My motel consisted of a row of huts, standing along the unpaved verge of what seemed to be the town's only street. I was
beginning to get used to the width of American streets, but this
one—which was large enough to swallow a four-lane highway—
was the most extravagant waste of land that I'd yet seen.

But then, what would have been the point of saving land,
when there was so much of it going spare? With an average of
only 60 people per square mile—compared with nearly 600 per
square mile in the British Isles—the main streets of most American towns could have been made as wide as football-grounds
without anyone noticing the loss of land. Indeed, it might have
given people a welcome excuse to use their cars to cross the
road; they seemed to use them for just about every other errand
—apart from in city centres, it was rare to see an American
walking.

This particular wide street had only one car on it and, in the
distance, one bicycle, carrying a small boy who, riding perilously
along the bumpy grass verge, was throwing newspapers on to the
porches of the houses. The houses were all of wood, and mostly
only one-storey; as usual, they had no gardens, but were surrounded, inside their picket fences, by worn, patchy grass, the
dusty monotony of which was relieved only by garden furniture
and an occasional swing or climbing frame. One front yard was
decorated by a sort of monstrous Christmas-tree made entirely
from the antlers of dead deer; several hundred of these, bleached
grey-white by sun and wind, were intertwined with all the precision of a formal arrangement of flowers. They towered high
above my head, a grisly monument to somebody's addiction to
the chase.

The whole town, in fact, had a greyish-whitish look. Only
the advertisement signs proclaiming—in brilliant scarlet, vermilion, emerald green, gold, or electric blue—the rival virtues of cigarettes, petrol, soft drinks, cafés or motels, added colour to the
scene; the signs, often higher than the houses, gave the town
something of the air of a minute elf village, built under the
shade of a patch of gaudy flowers.

But the sky—the sky had a blue so deep that it seemed to have
actual thickness, so that I felt that if I could rise into it I would
have to swim rather than fly; cloudless, featureless, it flowed
from horizon to horizon like a curving azure sea, illuminated by
a light so crystal-clear that there might not have been a single
mote suspended in the millions of miles that lay between my
eyes and the sun.

Miraculously—for I was still about 7,000 feet above sea-level—
my mountain sickness had vanished; I felt ravenously hungry,
and finding a vacant stool at the bar of a workmen's café,
recklessly ordered orange juice, cornflakes, coffee, and waffles
with bacon and maple syrup.

Pouring the sticky syrup lavishly over the buttery bacon-
decorated waffles it struck me that, apart from when I was feeling ill, the amount I was eating was getting a bit out of hand.

Breakfasts like the one I was eating today, mid-morning snacks of buns and Cokes, picnic lunches of hunks of ham and half-loaves of fresh bread, nibbles of apples and chocolate bars, suppers of anything and everything I could lay my hands on—I'd never guessed that bicycling would make me so hungry. I kidded myself that all the exercise I was taking would burn up the calories, but I had a sneaky feeling that I wasn't exactly getting thinner.

An old man on the next stool at the breakfast bar eyed my order with interest; he was wearing an oil-stained denim boiler suit and the pores of his heavily-lined face were pitted with grime.

"Travelling far?" he asked, as if hazarding a guess at the reason for my hunger.

"I'm on a bike trip."

He thought about this for a few moments, silently reaching for sugar to put into his coffee. The chrome cover of the glass sugar-jar had a sliding section that moved back to release the grains; his large, broken-nailed thumb fumbled clumsily at the slide, giving him, unexpectedly, the pathetic air of a backward child struggling to unwrap a piece of candy. Then—

"Where'you start from?"

"Virginia."

"Thought you must have been raised out east." And he smiled shyly, as if gratified that his guess had been proved right but at the same time reluctant to show pride in his own sagacity.

I was on the point of saying that I wasn't actually *from* Virginia, when it dawned on me that I was by now so far from the Atlantic that it was quite possible that the inhabitants of this isolated little town might find a Virginian accent as foreign as an English one. It seemed more polite to let him go on thinking I was a Virginian rather than to tell him that he was wrong, so I just went on eating.

Finally mastering the slide of the sugar-jar, the old man directed a small avalanche of white grains into a cup of milky coffee; as he stirred the now-glutinous liquid, a button detached itself from the cuff of his boiler suit, and fell, with the small plop! of a rising minnow, into the beige depths.

"Gosh darn," said the old man, mildly, fishing about with a small plastic spoon. Then, as if to excuse the behaviour of the button, he went on, "My wife died, six months past."

I made a small noise of commiseration.

"Yup," he said, as if agreeing to something that I had not, in fact, said. "Sure do miss her. Forty years, and never a night apart. Except when I had to go to hospital—hernia, that was."

Locating the button, he scooped it out of the coffee, and put it down on the throw-away plastic plate that had, until a few minutes before, supported his breakfast doughnut. A drop of coffee, spreading outwards from the tuft of thread attached to the shank of the button, marked the white polystyrene with a star-shaped pattern that might almost have been a tear.

Hastily I said, "What do you do, here?"

"Got my own engineering works, right next door. Care to come and visit, when you've finished your feed?"

I had an instant vision of unpacking my kit, to find a needle and thread. I hardened my heart; it was still, after all, a long way to the Pacific.

As I bicycled out of the town, heading, at this part of the journey, almost due north, I saw my breakfast companion standing—looking distressingly lonely—at the door of his "engineering works." It was a small corrugated-iron hut, almost hidden among a jumble of rusty machinery parts and tractors so old that I doubted if they would ever run again. He raised his hand in a farewell gesture; I wished—too late—that I had made time to sew on that button.

COLORADO (3)

If you ever want to be enchanted by skylarks the place to go is not Shelley's English countryside but the wild, watery plains that separate the mountain ranges of western Colorado. Around me as I bicycled along the rolling road on the far side of the Rockies lay miles of deserted scrub-land, intersected by marshy-looking streams; ragged barbed-wire fences outlined enclosures so enormous that I could only just make out where they began and ended, the white-faced Hereford cattle that wandered through them often so far from the road that they showed up only as reddish-brown dots, outlined indistinctly against distant, tufty patches of wind-stunted trees. Along each horizon, to my right and left, lay mountain ranges, at first blue and then—on their higher peaks—white and majestic under their still-unmelted winter snow. Occasionally I could see the outlines of wooden farm buildings, grouped as tightly as chickens round their red-roofed mother-hen farmhouses.

The farms were all set back a mile or so from the road, joined to it by rough tracks guarded, at their junction with the tarmac, by metal cattle-grids. Over the entrance to each track a simple arch—usually two stripped tree-trunks joined by a wooden cross-bar—carried a board on which was carved the name of the farm. Silver Sage Ranch, Lazy S Ranch (the S carved horizontally, to show exactly how lazy it was), Dry Creek Ranch (why did anyone choose to build a ranch *there*?), Tumbleweed Ranch (easy to see how that one got its name—great balls of tumbleweed, looking like giant pot-scrubbers, were bowling about all over the place), and occasionally one that must surely have perpetuated the name of some wife or sweetheart—Mary-Lou Ranch, Abigail Ranch,—or, poignantly, Last Resting-place.

The spring growth had not yet begun, and everything—the scrubby fields, the verges of the road, the sedgy outlines of the creeks, the low rolling mounds of the distant foothills—was a uniform dun brown, broken only by paler beige patches of dried-up grass and the vertical brownish bristles of the leafless, dwarfish trees. It would have been a distinctly bleak and depressing place, but for the incredible blue of the sky—reflected all around in the water of the creeks and marshes, so that the entire plain seemed to be scattered with a mosaic of lapis lazuli—and, of course, the larks. Hovering so high as to be out of sight, they poured down a cascade of glittering song, and as I passed from the territory of one bird to the next, the changing patterns of melody seemed to carry me effortlessly along the road; I felt dancer-light, totally free, and outrageously happy.

"Oh, pardon," said the fat woman sitting on the side of the road. Coasting recklessly round a blind corner, I had nearly run over her feet. They were encased in a pair of old baseball boots; the rest of her was wrapped in a pink-and-white spotted house-dress, against which her heavy breasts strained like two over-inflated footballs. "Pardon—we shouldn't have parked right here. But the kids had to go to the bathroom—you know how it is with kids." And she laughed merrily, the black curls of her un-tidy hair bouncing like springs on her plump polka-dotted shoulders.

Bathroom? I looked around, wondering if I'd unexpectedly reached some road-side motel. But for miles in every direction there was nothing to be seen but the burnt-up wasteland. Oh yes, of course—bathroom. By now I really should have grown used to the American euphemism. With what I hoped was an acceptable degree of tact, I feigned interest in Daisy's handle-bars while, one, two, three, four and then a fifth child popped up from behind the tussocks of grass, zipping up jeans or pulling up knickers according to sex. Finally, from behind a small hillock, the father of the family appeared; he was very tall, with the loose-jointed look of the cowboy heroes of almost any early Western, and his eyes seemed to match exactly the blue of the sky.

We all moved further down the road, to a safer parking place; the family station-waggon, which at first refused to start, responded to the combined pushes of the four bigger children and, steered on to the verge, proved to be a positive cornucopia of chocolate-chip cookies, apples and Cokes. I contributed some imitation butterscotch—the packet stamped Wee Glen Genuine Scottish Candy—and we all sat munching in the sunshine. The inevitable question wasn't long in coming.

"Where'you headin' for?"

By now I had fallen into a subterfuge—rather than say that I was aiming for the Pacific, I would name as my destination some relatively near point without—unless absolutely cornered—disclosing that it would only be a stopping-off place on a much longer journey. This was not only because people in the eastern states had, when I had said openly that I was planning to cross the continent on my bicycle, simply thought I was joking, but also because, as I neared the centre of America, they sometimes seemed to think that I was saying that I was going to the Pacific in order to conceal my true destination.

"Go on, quit kidding," they would say. "Tell us where you're *really* going." And if I insisted that I really was heading for Oregon, I occasionally sensed a slight atmosphere of disquiet, as if I puzzled them—and they didn't enjoy being puzzled. So, I now said that I was thinking of having a look at Old Faithful. The geyser was, in fact, something I very much wanted to see, and lay only about a hundred miles to the north.

"Keep meanin' to take the kids up there. Mebbe we will, some summer."

The children squirmed, and yelled approval; they all seemed to be roughly the same age, which I found puzzling.

"Any of you twins?" I asked, rescuing my bicycle-pump from the marginally smallest boy, who was trying to fit its nozzle into the ear of his younger sister. A chorus of negation, overlaid with howls of laughter, smothered this apparently preposterous suggestion.

"Naw, naw—I'm the eldest, then there's Gary, then David, and then. . . ."

Already I'd lost track of who was who, so I plunged in hastily with another question.

"And where are you going?"

"To git the groceries. And mebbe some shoes for Mary Sue."

Mary Sue, who looked about four, flopped over on to her back and held her feet in the air, exhibiting rather a lot of grubby knicker.

"My feet just grows and grows," she announced proudly.

"Where d'you go for groceries, round here?" I'd wondered how families in these sparsely-populated areas did their shopping. The mother named a town that I hadn't been planning to reach for another two days.

"But isn't that awfully far?"

"Lordy, no. Only about 70 miles."

Seventy miles? Just to do a bit of shopping? She laughed at what must have been my obvious amazement.

"Why, that's nothing. Henry here," and she poked a loving finger into her husband's stomach, "Henry here, he'll drive a hundred miles easy on a Saturday, just to git a bit of fishing."

Henry grinned happily. "Lovely fishing up in the mountains," he volunteered. "Trout as big as this." And he made the traditional gesture, hands held mendaciously far apart.

The children fell about, shrieking with glee. "Bigger'n that, Pa. Big as this." And they stretched their arms even wider, measuring fish the size of sharks.

"No, kids, that's enough. Don't you go teasing your Pa. Bad enough, spilling his night crawlers."

Night crawlers? I'd seen advertisements for them tacked up in many rural shop-windows. Night crawlers—so much a dozen.

They sounded so unspeakably horrible that even my insatiable
curiosity to see everything hadn't given me the courage to find
out exactly what they were. Dimly, I imagined a cross between a
leech and a wire-worm, humping its way with incandescent eyes
through darkness unilluminated by either moon or stars. Tentatively, I asked, "Have you got any? Night crawlers? I'd love to
see them." Liar, I told myself, under my breath.

"Nope. Sorry. Did have some, all ready for fishing." So that's
what they were—some sort of bait. "But the kids spilt 'em. Have
to git some more, Saturday." Thank heavens, I thought, re-
prieved from a confrontation that I secretly dreaded.

With much laughing and wriggling and shoving for places,
the family piled back into their station-waggon. But they hadn't
driven more than a hundred yards before they stopped and
reversed to where I was standing—one foot on a pedal—prepar-
ing to bicycle after them.

"Jes' thought—would you like a ride?"

The station-waggon wasn't the usual huge American affair,
but a compact, European-sized one, already wildly over-filled. Pa
and the two bigger boys were on the front seat, while Ma sat in
the back with the two smaller boys and Mary Sue who, cradled
on her mother's lap, had already fallen into a thumb-sucking
doze. But the idea of covering, in maybe two hours, a distance
that I had expected would take two days, was irresistible.
Wedged between the two boys on the front seat, Daisy tied to
the roof-rack with a scaringly frayed piece of string, I peered out
through the dust-hazed windscreen. Two mangy bison, penned
in a roadside stockade, peered morosely back. Roadside notices
flashed past, warning of OPEN RANGE—LOOSE STOCK. A
jagged board, slung like an inn-sign, announced that we were
LEAVING COLORFUL COLORADO, and was followed
swiftly by one which told us we were WELCOME TO BIG
WONDERFUL WYOMING. Signposts reeled by, pointing to
places familiar—if only by name—to a whole generation of European film-goers and television watchers. Saratoga. Laramie.

Why had I always thought of cowboy country as being dry

and rocky? Could it have been because it was easier—and more picturesque—to film in craggy locations than it would have been to struggle in this boggy, comparatively featureless desert? Later, I was also to confess to a Montana friend that many Britons still thought that the American west was peopled with cowboys and Indians wearing nineteenth-century clothes. "Don't worry," she told me consolingly, "there's plenty of east-coast Americans who think so too."

The shopping town, when we finally reached it, seemed much the same as the town where I had spent the previous night, except that it had two wide streets instead of one. They were on different levels, joined by steep, dusty side-streets on which stood the usual assortment of parked cars and rubbish-bins. It must have been garbage-collection day, for round the bins lay items that the owners hadn't been able to push inside; it didn't look a rich town, but the inhabitants were evidently well-off enough to throw away a stout kitchen chair, whose only fault seemed to be that someone had painted it a particularly vivid shade of puce, an apparently perfect—if slightly old-fashioned —refrigerator, and shoes that I would happily have walked away in, if I hadn't already replaced the ones I had ruined in the Rockies.

Some dark-eyed, straight-haired Indian children were queueing outside a battered iron door; it opened and, curious, I followed them inside. Beyond the door there was a ticket-kiosk, and beyond again a small concrete-floored roller-skating rink. The children, although noticeably poorly dressed, appeared to be quite happy to pay out what seemed to me a lot of money to skate round and round the shabby, airless rink. They circled apathetically, seeming almost mesmerised by their own rotating motion; above them four loudspeakers, suspended from the iron girders of the roof, belched out deafening pop music.

I came out of the skating-rink just in time to see a swarthy-looking man ride away down the street on Daisy. Normally I never left her for even a minute without padlocking her, but I hadn't planned to follow the children, and had forgotten. The

man was already several hundred yards away—I'd never catch
him now.

But what was this? He was turning back—he was riding
straight back towards me, grinning all over his face. And who
were these other swarthy men, who seemed to have materialised
out of the pavement? They were clapping and shouting as if the
man on Daisy was doing a circus turn; as he drew near he took
both hands off the handlebars and rode triumphantly up to the
group, showing all the happy pride of a small boy who has managed to complete his first lap without stabilisers. I reached Daisy
just as a second man leapt on and made ready to pedal off.

Now, Daisy had a great many good points—she was extremely
light, totally rust-proof, and folded easily. But she also had some
disadvantages—she was individualistic, temperamental, and easily damaged. All the way across the continent I had had to discourage people from trying her out, and the one thing she absolutely did not need now, if she was going to live to finish the
trip, was a buzz round the block under what appeared to be a
sixteen-stone gorilla.

"Stop!" I yelled, seizing the back of her seat. The man simply
stood on the pedals.

"No! No!" I yelled, dragged along on my heels as he started
to get up speed. The group on the pavement was now laughing
uproariously, as if the rider and I were some sort of comedy act.

"Stop thief!" I howled, throwing myself forward and clasping
the rider round his waist. My compass, which I wore on a cord
round my neck, fell forward, the cord entangling in the spokes
of the rear wheel. We skidded to a halt.

"Aargh!" I gasped, clutching at the wheel in a desperate attempt to avoid strangulation. All the men started talking at
once in a language that I didn't at first recognise. Then it
dawned on me that they were speaking Spanish. Mexican immi-
grants, I thought, wildly searching my mind for the Hispanic
equivalent of Cut the String, You Damn Fool. Then someone
produced a murderous-looking knife and started sawing at the
cord at a point exactly over my jugular vein.

"Calmese, calmese," another Mexican murmured soothingly, stroking my face with fingers that appeared to have had recent intimate contact with a chihuahua's lunch. Someone else imprisoned my hands while the cord was cut; I lay back in the gutter and thankfully breathed in gulps of cold Wyoming air.

Later, like birds on a telegraph wire, the Mexicans and I sat in a row along a brick wall, munching slices of a spicy, gristly sausage and trying to find some language in which we could communicate.

We drew primitive maps in the dust of the gutter. "England," I said. "Inglaterra. Londres." "Ah si!" they answered, cheerfully outlining a representation of the skyline of Manhattan. "No," I said, replying with a sketch of Buckingham Palace and what I felt was a staggeringly gifted portrait of the Queen, complete with crown. "Ah ha!" they cried, pointing to the crown and making circling motions over my head. "No, I'm positively no relation," I protested, pulling my pockets inside out to emphasise not only my non-regal status but also my even less regal resources.

Somebody cut up another sausage, even spicier and more gristly than the first. I had heard a rumour that Mexican sausages were made of a mixture of donkey and rabbit, in the proportion of one donkey to one rabbit; looking at my slice, I wondered if I'd got one of the hooves. Someone else peeled a shrivelled orange—splitting the skin with nails like the tines of a rusty harrow—and, placing it on a grimy handkerchief, offered it to me with all the panache of a ballet-dancer presenting a rose. The man who had cut my compass cord tried to splice the severed ends and, failing, sliced a strip from his own belt and fashioned me a leather thong, on which the compass swung far better than it had on the cord.

I got away fairly smartly after lunch, but once clear of the town I stopped and sat down to work out where I would go next. One of the beauties of this journey was that I didn't have to stick to any set route—provided that I hit the Pacific somewhere north of San Francisco, and that I reached Portland before the expiry-date of my return ticket, I could go anywhere I wanted. And Portland, according to my calculations, was exactly 1,008 miles away from where I was now sitting.

One thousand and eight miles—why, if my original estimate of 4,200 miles for the entire trip had been more or less right, I'd covered more than three-quarters of it already, in well under three-quarters of the available time. Perhaps, I thought, I could allow myself the luxury of a little side-trip. I got out all my remaining maps and spread them round me.

As well as a small-scale map that showed me my position relative to the rest of the world, I had started the trip with twenty large-scale automobile-type maps of the United States, covering a sweep from the Atlantic to the Pacific, and I say "remaining" because, so as to keep weight down to a minimum, I had been filling an envelope each week with the sections that I had passed through, and posting them home. Into the envelope—which had to be the very largest I could find—I also tucked used guide-books, picture postcards, addresses of people who had be-friended me, and any other bits of paper that I didn't actually want to lug along with me but which I wanted to keep. Exposed photo-films I posted straight to an English processing firm, tell-ing them to send the prints to my home address; it would have been hopeless to try to get them developed as I travelled, for I was never in one place long enough.

The automobile maps covered a lot of country to both north and south of my most direct route, and sitting in the sunshine, my back against a warm rock, I mulled over the rival merits of the roads that I could take, feeling again the sense of exhila-rating freedom that came from being able to do exactly as I pleased. There I was, completely alone; nobody knew where I was; I could go wherever I wanted without consulting anyone else, without making any concession to anyone else's personality or wishes; it was a type of freedom unknown in my past life, where almost every action had been conditioned by the needs—either physical or psychological—of somebody else. Perhaps eventually such total freedom might pall, but at that instant it was wonderful.

In spite of the warmth of the spring sun, the land around me still had a barren, wintry look, and no matter how hard I listened, I could hear no sound of any kind. Far back down the road, the town showed only as a pimple-like rash, breaking out from the tanned stubble of the sage. Then, down the railway track that, at this point, ran parallel to the road, an engine hooted mournfully, as if enquiring if there was anyone alive in the world. Slowly, a train snaked into sight—a hundred or so goods wagons stencilled with UNION PACIFIC AND SANTA FE. The names held for me all the magic of another age; it was as if history was rolling past me and I wouldn't have been surprised, at that moment, to have seen the Deadwood Stage rumble down the road, or glimpse a rider of the Pony Express galloping past, his leather chaps blackened with the sweat of his lathered horse.

The train ground away, clanking wearily, and when it had gone the silence seemed so complete as to be almost supernatural. Then I heard a car approaching; as usual in this sort of rolling terrain, it was audible while still invisible. I looked forward down the tarmac, and then backward the way I had come, finally spotting what looked like a small red lady-bird dipping in and out of sight as it negotiated the humps and hollows of the road. After it had passed me I could, for long minutes, still hear it as it buzzed away; in the still air, the sound lingered pervasively, so that had I not known that the car had just passed me I wouldn't have been able to decide if it was coming or going.

A duck hawk landed on a fence-post not four yards from where I was sitting, regarded me arrogantly from yellow, wide-irised eyes, then, with its menacingly curved beak, nonchalantly set about grooming its tail feathers. Suddenly it swivelled its head, rose on decisive wings, banked steeply, and dived talons-first into the brush. There was a brief shrill squeak, like chalk

drawn across a blackboard, and the hawk rose again, bearing in
its talons the still-struggling body of a Whitetail prairie dog.

I turned my attention back to my maps. Just where was I
going next? The most obvious way to head would have been
north-west, towards Portland, at an angle that would—if I pur-
sued it for about 3,000 miles—take me into Alaska. But as I was
making such good time, I decided to travel instead almost due
west, and then veer south-west into Utah. This would give me a
chance to see Salt Lake City, even though it would mean that
later on, so as to reach Yellowstone Park, I would have almost
to retrace my steps by bicycling due north.

I jumped on to Daisy and set off towards the land of the Mormons. Everything in the world seemed quite remarkably cheerful—not only was the weather staying fine but on that very open
road I was getting more than my usual ration of whistles.

Weeks of non-stop exercise had done wonders for my legs,
and constant exposure to the sun had lightened my normally
mouse-coloured hair so that, seen from the back, I must have ex-
uded something of the irresistible allure of a centre-forward
from a reform-school hockey team. At any rate, grossly sex-
starved men, overtaking my bicycle from behind in cars or lorries,
would let out suggestive cries of unbridled lust, which turned,
after they had passed me and had realised—too late—that I was
quite literally old enough to be their mother, to such expressions
of disappointment that I was tempted to tie a notice to the small
of my back, saying "Don't Bother."

But if I ignored the sad looks on their departing faces, the initial wolf-whistles were rather cheering; besides, I had just passed
a signpost that proclaimed that it was only 108 miles to the next
town. I had no idea what the town would be like, but it had a
most attractive name.

WYOMING (1)

In America, as in Europe, bicycles aren't allowed on the big
inter-state roads; an exception is made, though, when these
roads are positively the only way of getting from one place to another, a concession that isn't necessary in, for instance, England,
where there is always some alternative Celtic or Early Roman
track down which the lowly bicyclist can creep.

The road I was now on seemed to be the only one that
crossed the rather blank bit of map that lay ahead; it looked like
the sort of highway that would, in a thickly populated bit of
country, have been banned to bicyclists, but I couldn't see any
notices forbidding me to use it, so I took a chance and continued along it.

Perhaps this is as good a moment as any to confess that I
never managed to work out what some American road-signs
meant. In particular, the one that had the outline of a bicycle
on it baffled me; did it mean Special Track for Bicycles, or Bicycles Forbidden? I tried several times to get an information
leaflet—or indeed anything that would tell me what the various
signs meant—but nobody whom I asked seemed to know of any
such thing, so after a while I gave up asking, and simply treated
all signs with a certain wariness.

This road—which didn't seem to have any signs—was bordered with a two-strand wire fence, beyond which the arid land,
roughened with stunted sage-brush, stretched out to distant

stratified escarpments; I had the impression that on the far side of the escarpments the view would be exactly the same—more barren land, more sage, more escarpments. Could it have been around here, I wondered, that dinosaur bones had been found? It certainly looked the right sort of terrain for digging up the skeleton of a pterodactyl or tyrannosaurus rex, for the wind, with its massive powers of erosion, would have done much of the work already—if the height of the flat-topped knolls that dotted the landscape was anything to go by, the original surface-level of the region must have been at least a hundred feet above the present one. The rocky caps that had prevented these large knolls being eroded in pace with the land that surrounded them gave the knolls the look of monstrous pepper-pots, abandoned on the deserted land at the end of some gigantic prehistoric feast.

Direction signs pointed to such inhospitable-sounding places as Bitter Creek and Red Desert. The lettering on the signs was very big, presumably so that drivers—all of whom seemed to be driving unusually fast, as if wanting to get out of the locality as soon as possible—could read the signs in time to slow down enough to make the turn. The size of the signs seemed totally out of keeping with the condition of the tracks down which they pointed, which were mostly unmetalled and honeycombed with uncomfortable-looking potholes. I didn't feel tempted to turn down any of the tracks, not so much because of the names on the signs but because I couldn't see even a single house anywhere along them.

I passed a small group of caravans, huddled together a hundred yards from the main road; a weary-looking girl was strolling dejectedly down the track that led to them, a screaming toddler clinging to one of her hands. The other hand held an open can of beer from which, at every third or fourth step, she took a bored, perfunctory swig. The paint on the caravans was peeling, and the dogs that tore down to the road to bark at me had, behind their bluster, a furtive air, retreating, tails tucked in, when I shouted at them to go home. The main road just went on and on without, it seemed, any further human habitation from here to eternity. An oil-derrick raised its mournful head above the sage, pumping lugubriously; more and more appeared, their heads moving relentlessly, like those of a flock of insatiably browsing locusts. A huge pipe snaked alongside the road, running apparently from nowhere to nowhere. As far as I could see in every direction, there was nothing even remotely like a house, and when the sun finally vanished and a strong, cold wind got up, there was no alternative but to camp exactly where I was. On my own.

I tried to remember a few of the basic rules about camping in the wilds. "Climb a tree"—the biggest tree in sight was all of three feet tall, and wouldn't have discouraged any marauder larger than a mouse. "Don't camp near running water"—well, that rule was easy to obey; there wasn't so much as a puddle for miles. "Hammer your tent-pegs securely home"—the ground was like concrete, overlaid with the sort of stuff that collects at the bottom of very old biscuit-tins. "Be sure to position your tent with the opening facing downwind"—the wind, unco-operatively, seemed to be blowing from all points of the compass at once.

I lay curled in my sleeping-bag, listening to the oil-derricks nagging at the moon. Pump-thump. Pump-thump. Pump-thump. At first, remembering the ticking clock that a vet had advised me to put in the basket of a newly weaned puppy, I managed to convince myself that they sounded like maternal heart-beats, but after the moon went down the noise developed a distinct resemblance to the footfalls of cyclopian giants, and in the very dark hour just before dawn—when I was not only frightened but also astoundingly cold—the skeletons of dinosaurs slid out of the escarpments and padded menacingly round my tent, grinding their terrible tombstone teeth.

No druid on midsummer's day can have watched for the first rays of the sun more eagerly than I did. As its first quadrant edged over the horizon the next morning, I cautiously unzipped the door of my tent; in the almost-horizontal rays, each dry

blade of grass seemed like a tiny golden spear, planted stiffly at
the base of its own attenuated shadow. I edged myself out of the
tent and stood up, my own shadow unrolling from my feet like
the trail of bent daisy-heads that ribbons a lawn in the wake of a
well-struck croquet-ball. The dinosaurs had vanished, and in
their place, not fifty yards away, stood a small herd of Prong-
horn antelopes. The antelopes turned their graceful heads and
regarded me with expressions of utter disbelief.

I stood completely still, hoping to persuade them that I was
harmless, but after a moment they turned and fled, their small
hooves tapping the ground with a noise like an officeful of type-
writers. A few hundred yards away they suddenly halted, dropped
their heads, and began feeding as if nothing had happened; the
camouflage of their pale tan hides was so perfect that if I hadn't
noticed where they had stopped I wouldn't have been able to
see them.

The larks were at it again, of course—whoever coined the
phrase "up with the lark" certainly knew what he was talking
about, for now, even though half the sun was still below the horizon, a whole gang of them were already yelling their beaks off
somewhere up out of sight in the sky. Except in a few places—
one of which, curiously, is Hawaii—the New World doesn't
have European-type skylarks. These were probably Horned
Larks, so called because of the tufts of black feathers on their
heads, but they were too high up for me to identify with any cer-
tainty.

I sat in the door of my tent, my sleeping-bag cuddled round
my shoulders, and drank the coffee that I had brewed up on my
tiny camping stove. This stove burnt small lozenges of solid
fuel, which would ignite even when wet, and packed neatly inside its own billycan; the only snag was that the billycan (which
also served as a saucepan) was the only "cup" that I carried and,
being made of thin aluminium, conducted heat so fast that if
the liquid inside was acceptably hot the rim felt like a branding-
iron. At the beginning of the trip I had either burnt my mouth
on the hot metal or resigned myself to drinking tepid coffee, but

by now I had worked out how to drink during the fleeting instant when the cup was cool enough to touch but the liquid inside was still comfortingly hot, and my breakfasts were considerably more enjoyable.

I had completely abandoned any conventional ideas about either the times at which meals should be eaten or the type of food which should be eaten at any particular meal; except when I was with other people, I ate at any convenient time between feeling the first pangs of hunger and actually collapsing, and the ingredients of each meal were whatever I happened to have with me. I usually carried bread, cheese, oranges, a plastic bottle of water, a tin of instant coffee, and some chocolate—I had read somewhere that one could bicycle about seven miles on one ounce of chocolate. These, of course, were emergency rations— for use when camping, or when unexpectedly picnicking. If I was anywhere near a café, I would, as I have said earlier, tear in and hoover up everything I could lay my hands on, and even my emergency rations were frequently supplemented by ham, fresh vegetables, and other goodies.

Today, my breakfast was made up of coffee, the remains of a raw cauliflower, half a packet of potato crisps, and some peanut butter eaten—because I wanted to husband my small reserve of bread—off the end of my finger. Delicious, I thought, licking my finger and then wiping it on what I imagined was a smooth white rock. Then I took another look at the "rock." It wasn't a rock at all, but the bleached skull of a Bighorn sheep. I struck camp with a speed that would have done credit to a Queen's Scout; as I rolled up my tent, the skull's empty eye sockets gazed at me with haunting loneliness.

It took me thirty-six more hours to reach the desert town with the attractive name: surprisingly, it had a very luxurious motel. Thirty minutes after I had registered—and it says a lot for the management that they accepted someone who must have looked as if she had been left over from a re-make of *Tarzan and the Ape Woman*—I was swimming in a glass-walled heated pool. I'd had a normal bath first; the bath-tub, incidentally, had been so highly polished that I had had to leave a fluffy towel trailing over the edge so that a tiny spider, who had had the misfortune to fall in just after I had let the water run away, could climb out.

I sat on the balcony of my fourth-floor room, drinking iced beer out of a tooth-glass that I'd popped out of a drum-tight cellophane sheath stamped Sanitised for Your Convenience. The same words were printed on the paper band that was draped—like a Miss World sash—over the lavatory seat.

The motel was a mile or so outside the town, and was surrounded by even flatter and more arid country than that which I had just crossed. All I could see from my high balcony was a petrol station, a small village of mobile homes, some telegraph poles, and a pale road, lying like a fallen washing-line across the sandy terrain. Cars passed monotonously down the road, their shapes, colours and types so repetitive that I felt I was watching one of those mechanised Christmas shop-window displays, where reindeer and sledges, glued to a circular moving band, follow each other endlessly through a curving landscape of cotton-wool snow. Night fell, the tinted pinpricks of light from the caravans combining with the scarlet rear lamps of the moving cars to reinforce the impression that it was time to hang up my stocking.

But my stockings—or, to be more exact, my socks—were soaking in a billowing detergent foam, surrounded by all my other clothes. I had stopped at the motel restaurant on my way up from the pool and eaten an enormous meal of steak, salad, baked potato, apple-pie and ice cream, so I didn't have to leave my room again, which was just as well, considering that all I would have had to wear would have been the counterpane off the king-size bed.

It was six o'clock next morning when I went downstairs, and the motel coffee-shop hadn't yet opened, so I bicycled back into the town, looking for the bus station—bus stations, I'd found, were usually good hunting-grounds for coffee, no matter what the hour.

The familiar sign of a racing greyhound was suspended from

the wall of a sleazy-looking hotel. I pushed the worn brass handle of a swing door and went in. At the back of what might once have been the hotel dining-room, a cynical-looking blonde of uncertain age leant on a stained wooden counter; thumb-tacked to the wall behind her, posters urged me to SEE AMERICA THE LUXURY WAY, and a smaller sign, standing on the counter, invited me to insure myself against Unforseen Demise Due to Accident. I asked if there was any coffee going.

"Nope."

Couldn't you squeeze out even the tiniest smile, I wondered, studying the way the blonde's mouth turned down at the corners. Then it struck me that I probably wasn't looking any too bright myself, and rearranged my face into what I hoped was a friendlier shape. The reaction was immediate.

"Could make you some, if you'd like."

At that moment the door was banged open and a tall, burly man strode in, positively radiating virility.

"Hi, beautiful!" he cried, leaning over the counter and grabbing the blonde round the waist. "How's my best girl this morning?"

She twisted round to face him, holding the hot coffee-pot at arm's length as he planted an uninhibited kiss on the vermilion lipstick of her mouth. Noticing me standing further along the counter, he gave a conspiratorial wink.

"Got to keep the hired help happy, haven't we?" he said, laughing. The blonde pushed him away, chuckling delightedly.

The door swung open again, and two straggle-haired youths slouched in, the collars of their luridly-checked lumber-jackets turned up against the chill of the early morning air. They thumbed some quarters into a slot-machine, extracted two bottles of Coke, and slumped down on a delapidated sofa.

"Don't you go bringing those bottles on the bus, mind now," said the burly man, releasing his hold on the blonde.

One of the youths put up a token show of rebellion. "Who says?"

"I say. And I'm the driver, ain't I?" He turned to me and, as if to justify his authoritativeness, added, "Empties in the luggage-rack, they bounce around like bugs in a blanket. Use 'em to hit the driver too—some folks," he added, under his breath, eyeing the young men suspiciously.

The blonde handed two cups of coffee across the counter; there was a miniature whirlpool in the centre of each, where she had stirred in the sugar.

"How much do I owe you?" I queried, fishing in the pocket of my jeans.

"Aw, let me treat you—I was going to perk some up for Muscle Man anyway. No, no, really—it's my pleasure."

The bus driver extended a grey-shirted arm over the top of a glass display cabinet, slid back a section that faced towards the service side of the counter, and extracted a doughnut.

"You travelling with me?" he asked, biting into the sugar-dusted circle.

I shook my head. "I'm bicycling."

"Is that so? Which way are you heading?"

"Salt Lake City."

He put down his coffee cup, and wiped his mouth on the back of his hand. Some lipstick, that had been transferred from the blonde's mouth to his own, smudged his sunburnt knuckles. He rubbed it off with the palm of his other hand.

"Lady," he said, with weighty consideration. "If you want to get to Salt Lake City, you'd sure better ride with me. Ain't no way you can make that trip on a bicycle. Hundred'n eighty-one —maybe hundred'n eighty-two miles, that trip. I should know— do it 'most every day."

"I think I'll try."

"Please yourself. I'll stop and pick you up if I spot you— tomorrow or the next day. If the rattlers ain't got you." And he laughed gleefully at his own joke, holding his cup out for a second fill.

Outside, as I checked Daisy's brakes, the door of the hotel swung open behind me, and one of the sloppy-looking youths lounged out; he rested his bottom against a fire-hydrant, and waited patiently until I straightened up. Then—

"You short?" he inquired.

I didn't know what he meant, and just looked at him, puzzled.

"Short—short of a dollar. Happy to treat you to the bus ticket, if you are."

"That's very, very nice of you. But I like biking—honestly."

The boy twisted the worn chrome bracelet of his watch, and glanced at the dial. "OK," he said, not at all perturbed. "I guess we'll be leaving shortly." He eased his bottom off the hydrant and strolled back to the door.

"I really do appreciate the offer," I called after him, worried that I might have sounded ungrateful.

He turned in the doorway and smiled. "See you," he said, making, with a hand held level with his shoulder, a circular polishing motion in the air.

WYOMING (2)

Seven o'clock on a bright Wyoming morning. My own shadow stretching far ahead of me down the road. The wheels of my little bicycle spinning as sweetly as the cogs of a well-adjusted Swiss watch. A nearby flock of sheep were pushing and shoving at each other as they foraged on the side of a scrubby ravine, and one sheep, turning his head to look up at me, fell over on to his back and got cast. I braked hurriedly and scrambled down the slope, knowing that a sheep, stuck on its back, can die of starvation.

"Just breathe deeply and try to relax," I counselled, getting a grip on a hank of his wool and attempting to roll him over on to his side. He was one of those black sheep that are put into flocks in a ratio of one to a hundred (one black sheep to each hundred white) so that shepherds can make rapid estimates of how many hot dinners they've got when they're too far away to count all the legs and divide by four. He kicked out spitefully with his back legs.

"Now, now—none of that," I said firmly, getting as far as possible from the sharp little hooves. The only bit of the sheep that seemed to be relatively incapable of doing me a damage was his head, so I transferred my grip to his neck; he let out a piteous bleat, and went as limp as an armful of wet laundry.

"Over we go!" I cried triumphantly, heaving him sideways. But he was heavier than I'd expected, and I lost my footing on the gritty slope; clasped swooningly in each other's arms, the sheep and I tobogganed to the floor of the ravine.

Fortunately this particular sheep was even more than ordinarily stupid; it took him quite a long time to work out what had happened, and while he was trying to think what to do next he lay almost motionless. I was getting my buttons quite satisfactorily unhooked from his wool when I happened to look upwards, towards the road. Peering over the verge was a small grey-haired man, wearing an old-fashioned jacket; beside him, clasping one hand apprehensively to her mouth, was a middle-aged lady in an outstandingly respectable felt hat. They looked just like the wooden figures that had—until he got at them with a toy hammer—been glued to the gangway of my grandson's Noah's Ark.

"Hello!" I shouted cheerily, imagining that, seeing Daisy lying on the side of the road, their Samaritan kindness had prompted them to investigate. "Very kind of you, but I'm quite all right."

The sheep, goaded to action by the sound of my voice, began to struggle convulsively. Silently, Mr. and Mrs. Noah gazed down at me, then they turned and looked at each other, both faces carrying a look of stunned horror. Obviously by common consent, they vanished out of sight, and moments later I heard the put-put of a small car accelerating off down the road.

Towards mid-day, after a ride serenaded by snow buntings, green-tailed towhees and pink-legged savannah sparrows, I turned off on to a side-road, and sat down by a river to enjoy a picnic. Much as I had always loved picnics with my family, it was a joy on this trip to be able to halt exactly where I wanted, without the usual discussions as to whether to stop *here*, or try for some possibly better place further on, and it was marvellous not to be in charge of anyone. Flopping blissfully on the grass, I realised how irritating I must have been on family outings—for ever pressing children to finish up their orange squash, so that I could rinse out the cups, or nagging them about putting the rubbish back into the picnic basket.

I feel pretty passionate on the subject of rubbish, and when travelling by car always take it home with me, but after the first few hundred miles on Daisy my views became a bit more flexible, and I began to ask myself questions. Everything, I argued to myself, came from the earth to begin with—including the silica that went into the glass bottles and the metals that made tins. Sooner or later—even if it took a million years—everything was going to be re-absorbed by the earth. If there was a rubbish-bin around, I naturally put my rubbish into it, but if I was picnicking miles from anywhere I simply dug a hole and buried it, scattering pebbles on top of the replaced earth in what I deluded myself was an imitation of a Japanese garden.

Before the rangers come after me, though, I had better quickly add that I never did this in national parks, where, because of the number of holiday visitors, I saw the point of the notices commanding Pack It In, Pack It Out. And I always took anything made of plastic along to the next town; plastics may originally have come out of the earth, but I had a feeling that the earth wasn't yet ready to have them call her Mother.

I spent longer than I should beside the river, first watching swirling drifts of flies fall victim to rising fish, then waiting to see if the great blue herons—their stick-legs almost perfect facsimiles of the reeds among which they stood—would in turn make a meal of the fish, and by the time I started off again the euphoria of the morning had rather worn off.

A hundred and eighty-two miles, I brooded, remembering what the bus-driver had told me. Maximum speed on Daisy, 15 miles an hour. Fifteen miles, incidentally, was the distance that the old covered waggons, heading for California in the 1849 Gold Rush, normally covered in a day, so although it sounds very slow to a car driver, it wasn't really a shaming hourly average for Daisy. But fifteen miles an hour was what she would do on a flattish road, in reasonable weather; if I allowed for walking up hills, taking photographs, and generally lolling around, her average was more like twelve, so I would really need three days to get to Salt Lake City—five hours being quite long enough, at a stretch, to perch on a small leather triangle pushing one's feet around in circles. And the same number again, to head back north. I suddenly realised that I hadn't got as much time in hand as I had thought. Passing an isolated homestead, I asked a woman what some distant mountains were called, so as to gauge my position on the map. She shrugged her shoulders.

"They'se just wilderness country," she said, much as a farmer might have said "That's corn," when one had hoped that he would identify the sprouting grain in his fields as wheat or oats or barley.

"Wilderness country"—the words seemed, in spite of the woman's abruptness, to hold a magic quality, as if the peaks might have been those of Ephel Duath—the Mountains of Shadow that ringed the land of Mordor. I bicycled on, lost in wonder at the rose-pink outlines of the mysterious wilderness.

Rose pink? What were they doing looking rose pink? Too late, I realised that it was because the sun had nearly set.

I'm afraid it may sound terribly improvident, but as I had never meant to travel after dark I hadn't fitted Daisy with lights; for once, this wasn't because of my passion for keeping the weight of my equipment down but because a dynamo set— which would have been the only logical one to have—would have stopped her folding up satisfactorily. On the rare occasions when I was still bicycling after sunset, I had to rely on reflectors to defend my back while, ahead, I shone the small pocket torch that I used for camping. The system was about as efficient as a bald toothbrush, and this evening, as the dusk deepened, I was distinctly happy to spot a lit-up café.

Right across the United States, roadside cafés had a predictable sameness. There would be a counter, fronted by a row of high stools, some plastic-topped tables, and benches with imitation-leather seats. Flashing neon signs, either in the uncurtained windows or on the roof, would advertise not only the opening hours but also the allegedly bargain price of the food. "7 A.M. TO 7 P.M." "ALL U CAN EAT FOR $1.50." "PIZZAS! PIZZAS! YOUR CHOICE OF FILLING." This particular

café appeared to have bought up the surplus stock of a zoo—
"JUMBO STEAKS," it announced proudly, the illuminated
words snaking down the convolutions of a twisted neon tube.
"JUMBO STEAKS! JUMBO STEAKS!"

A middle-aged man stood behind the counter, scraping, with
a metal slice, the top of an iron griddle.

"Yes?" he queried, without turning round. The back of his
neck was deeply lined; when he bent his head forward to check
the griddle the central crease showed pale against his sunburnt
skin, like the white crumb of a loaf exposed as the crust is sliced.

"May I have some coffee, please?"

He stopped scraping and stood completely still. Some pieces
of charred food fell back on to the hot griddle, where they siz-
zled and wriggled as if alive, giving off tiny explosions of blueish
smoke. Then he turned slowly round to face me. A hundred
years ago, I thought, a bartender might have turned in just such
a wary fashion, apprehensive in case an alien voice should signal
the need to reach for a gun.

At the far end of the bar a handsome tow-haired man put
down the knife with which he had been slicing a steak, picked
up a fork, and studied me curiously; strange, I thought, how the
pioneer shortage of knives had resulted in this now-unnecessary
national habit of slicing food first and then recoursing, for the
actual process of eating, to an unpartnered fork.

I drank some of the coffee; it tasted, as usual, of virtually
nothing. There was no sound except for the faint sizzling of the
griddle and the steady chomp-chomp of the steak-eater's jaws.

"Do you know if there's anywhere around here where I could
spend the night? A motel or something?"

"Nope."

"Any camping-ground, then? I've got a tent."

"Nope."

I felt discouraged, unwilling even to ask if I could camp in the
neighbourhood of the café, and, finishing the liquid in my cup,
went outside. To the west, the horizon was now outlined in
scarlet, as if Rome was burning just beyond the hills; to the east,

the first stars were pricking the navy-blue curtain of the advancing night.

Behind me, the door of the café opened, and then banged shut. The tow-haired man came towards me, walking with such an easy, relaxed gait that I half expected him to untether a horse.

"Could give you a ride down the road, if you'd like. Wouldn't be any worse off than you are here. Might even be better."

The imaginary horse turned suddenly into a huge truck, loaded with very large concrete boxes. Picking up Daisy as effortlessly as if she'd been a toddler's tricycle he lifted her on to the truck and, clambering up beside her, secured her between two of the concrete boxes. He swung himself round into the driver's seat, and, leaning over, opened the door of the passenger side.

"Jump in."

The base of the door was about on a level with my eyebrows, and in the gloom I could see no step to help me up. The wheel was enormous, the hub at the height of my hipbone; I managed to get one foot on it, and grabbed at a side-mirror. But where was I meant to put my other foot? I fell back again on to the ground, twisting my ankle as I landed. I threw myself forwards and upwards with all the determination of a Sherpa. One foot on the hub, the other scrabbling frantically on a sloping mudguard, a heave of the hand from the driver—and I was in.

"Ain't much accustomed to gettin' in trucks?" the driver asked, slipping the gear-lever nonchalantly from slot to slot. It seemed to be something of a rhetorical question, so I countered it with another.

"Know any motel or anything, this way?"

"Not between here and where I'm stoppin'. But you can sleep in back, if you like. In the load."

"That's very kind. What are you carrying?" The big concrete boxes were unlike anything I'd ever seen before.

"Vaults—funeral vaults."

"What?"

"Folks as haven't got family vaults. Bury these in the ground. Casket rests inside. Keeps out the water. Bugs too, I guess."

I really didn't know what to say next. The driver obviously thought I needed encouragement.

"They're snug, lady—real snug. I've slept in one many a time. 'Course, a regular casket's more comfortable—all that satin padding. But a vault—why, it's just like a regular little house, specially if you get the lid over about the half of it."

Frankly, the idea of having the lid half on did nothing to entice me.

"Perhaps I could put up my tent?"

"Please yourself. My young lady—that's where I'll be stoppin' —she's got a yard in back of her mobile home. Could put up a tent there, I guess."

Reaching up, he switched on a two-way radio; it was bolted to the roof just above the windscreen, and as he flicked the first switch a rough male voice came from the loudspeaker, giving information on road conditions. He flicked another switch, identified himself, and asked some questions in a sort of verbal shorthand.

"CB radio," he said, in answer to my own, unspoken, question. "Citizens' Band—most of us truckers use it. Like for company. And to warn each other, if the Smokies are out."

"Smokies?"

"Smokie Bears—the police. These radios, they've a pretty short range, but it's far enough. Weather, highway accidents, Smokies—that sort of thing. Some of the boys, they have a second set at home, so they can call up their wives."

"To let them know when to start cooking supper?"

"Or to give 'em time to kick their boy-friends out." He laughed happily, smacking the flat of his hand on the steering-wheel, as if it had been a bongo drum. "You got a boy-friend, lady?"

"Give me a chance—I've got three grandchildren."

"Can't see as how that makes a difference. My grandma, she had white hair—white as a bowlful of suds. Know what she used to say? She used to say it don't matter if there's snow on the mountains, just so long as there's warmth in the valleys. Married five times, my grandma. Dead now, God rest her."

"I'm sorry."

"Aw, you don't need to be sorry for my grandma. Called to her eternal rest in Vegas—heart attack, just after she got a jackpot up. Only thing she'll have been sorry for is not gettin' to spend all those silver dollars. Shucked out real silver dollars, those days."

The road streamed under the huge wheels, its sameness giving it the look of a grey conveyor belt, without beginning or end. I found myself dozing, the words of the driver blending into the roar of the engine.

I woke suddenly, to find we had pulled up on the edge of a group of caravans. The driver was already swinging himself to the ground.

"This is where I stop. Hang around, will you?"

I watched him as he strode down a makeshift alley; it was lit only by some bare electric bulbs strung on a looping wire, and as he walked he swerved from side to side to avoid inkily-shadowed potholes. I saw him climb—at one bound—the wooden steps that led up to the door of one of the caravans; he rapped confidently on a glass panel, the door was flung open, and he vanished inside, his arms wrapped round a female figure.

Silence fell, broken only by the whistle of the wind past the electric-light wire and the faint sound of a television. I peered around, trying to spot a place where I could pitch my tent; in the hostile darkness, the residual heat of the truck engine rose round my ankles, giving me the comforting illusion that I had the company of a dog. Just as I was beginning to wonder if he had forgotten me, the driver came back.

"My doll—my young lady—says she'll be happy to have you visit with her. OK? Here, I'll get your bicycle down. Now mind, don't you let on what I said about marriage—about us truckers being better off single. Me and her, we're getting married just as soon as her divorce comes through."

And he paused under a bare light-bulb, putting his finger to the side of his nose conspiratorially, unaware that I'd slept through his confidences about matrimony.

A woman leant against the open door of the caravan. She was wearing black toreador pants, high-heeled gold boots, and an elasticised lace blouse that clearly didn't have a bra under it; her blonde hair was teased into a halo round a pert face that, for all its wide-eyed little-girl look, was etched with faint, carefully powdered-over lines.

"You come right in, honey. The very idea of you sleeping outside—why, lover boy, you should be ashamed of yourself even thinkin' of it, when you know I've got the guest-room just waitin' for friends."

The caravan was surprisingly spacious. Everything in it shone with a combination of newness and polish; even the knobs of the clothes-washer in the kitchen—which was separated from the sitting-room by only a highly-glossed counter-top, on which the woman was already placing sandwiches—gleamed like guardsmen's buttons, while the artificial flames of the electric fire were reflected dazzlingly on the lacquered gilt legs of the marble-topped coffee-table. On the coffee-table stood a large cut-glass bowl, its facets only marginally less sparkling than the centre-piece of a Tiffany window.

Slouching among the velvet cushions of a spindle-legged sofa, Lover Boy looked even larger and more muscular than he had at the wheel of his truck; his cotton T-shirt clung to his spectacular torso, defining each pectoral and bicep as anatomically as if they had been covered only by a lick of paint. Doll was evidently having considerable difficulty in keeping her hands off him, and kept dashing out of the kitchen to give him a little pat or prod. Each time that she crossed the floor the high heels of her gold boots made little spiky indentations in the pile of the sitting-room carpet, like the marks left fleetingly in grass by the small sharp hooves of a goat.

"Now, you mustn't let us keep you up," she said coyly, whisking away my plate the instant I had finished eating and slotting it into a dish-washer so shiny that it appeared never to have been used. "You must be weary—all that travellin'."

Proudly she showed me the bathroom, its gleaming shelves clustered with apparently unopened containers of toilet-water, talcum powder, cleansing milk and hand-lotion. A chenille rug patterned to look like a sleeping Pekingese curved round the pedestal of the WC, and the shower-curtain that hung by the lavender-coloured bath was tied back with a spray of plastic orchids. Through the open door of the main bedroom I caught a glimpse of a satin-covered double bed, flanked on either side by china lamps with pink, lace-edged shades.

The spare room was at the end of a short corridor, and was about the size of a railway sleeper.

"I'll get you some sheets."

"Please—don't bother. I'll be quite all right in my sleeping-bag."

"Sure?"

Sure, I was sure—I was asleep even before the dish-washer had finished running.

I don't know what time it was that I woke up again, feeling unbearably thirsty. It must have been the salty filling in those sandwiches, I thought, groping for—and failing to find—a bedside light. I'll have to find the switch at the door, I thought, getting up.

The room was dark, with the kind of blackness that feels thick, like burnt toffee. I slid my feet along the floor, to avoid knocking anything over. Ah—here was the door. But which side was the switch? I patted around, but could feel nothing. All right then, I thought, I'll just open the door very quietly, pop on a shirt, and try to find a light in the bathroom.

But the door-handle didn't seem to want to turn. Perhaps it was the type that one pulled, rather than turned? I gave it a small tug. Nothing happened. I pulled the knob really hard. Quite silently the entire wall fell on top of me.

By now my eyes were getting accustomed to the dark, and I could make out a faint greyish oblong, which I thought must be

the window. Still supporting the wall, I balanced on one foot
and extended the other, waist high, in the direction of the window. A small tassle lodged itself helpfully between my toes and
with a bit of leg-work that would have dazzled the Bolshoi I
twitched the curtain open.

Now I could see—dimly—what had happened. I hadn't
grasped the handle of the door, but of a cupboard, and what had
fallen forward was the entire front section of a built-in wardrobe. Gingerly, I stepped backwards, so that I could look over
the top of the part that I was holding, and saw on the far side a
row of dresses in plastic dust-covers, and a shelf of hats in
matching plastic bags. Below were some metal rails, supporting
shoes as neatly paired as couples in a mass Chinese wedding.

I wondered whether I should call for help, but decided
against it—somehow I didn't feel that this would be Lover Boy's
favourite night for fixing the furniture, and on top of that I
feared that my story about wanting a glass of water might sound
a bit thin, compared to a possible alternative interpretation—
that I was taking advantage of Doll's kindness to rifle her cupboards. Gingerly, I pushed the wall up a little, and stretched out
my other leg to the light switch by the door.

After that, it was easy—except that I had actually to get inside
the cupboard to operate the little bolts that secured the wardrobe front to the ceiling of the caravan, and it was sort-of
cramped in there, among all those plastic dust-covers.

It wasn't until I was back inside my sleeping-bag that I realised that I'd never had the glass of water.

WYOMING, UTAH AND IDAHO

"Of course, the beauty business isn't what it was," said Doll sadly, lighting up her third cigarette. A plate bearing the smeared remnants of some scrambled eggs told me that Lover Boy had breakfasted well before leaving; he must have been an early riser, for there had been no sign of him when, around seven, I had woken up. Doll glanced forlornly out of the window at the empty space where his truck had been parked, and tapped the ash from her cigarette into the scraped-out skin of an orange. "Not what it was," she repeated, sighing.

"What's been the matter?"

"Too much do-it-yourself—home perms, all that trash. And the Natural Look. OK for kids—leaving their faces bare; trouble is, oldsters do it too—think it makes them look young. Doesn't of course—just makes them look like old coots with stripped skins." She reached for the coffee percolator. "Another cup?"

"Thanks."

"When I started, some of the girls'd get their hair fixed two-three times a week. Thought nothing of comin' in for a facial or a manicure in their lunch-hour. Now they just go and lie round in the sun, baking out their natural oils. I tell them it's pure death—look like a lot of old squaws by the time they're forty. But a girl of twenty, she doesn't even think there is a time when she'll be forty. Sounds like Deadsville, forty does, when you're twenty."

In the bright early morning sunshine, the tracery of lines round her mouth and eyes showed up with a cruel clarity. How old was she herself, I wondered. Forty-one? Forty-two? And Lover Boy? Thirty-five at the most.

"Where do you work, now?"

"Got my own place. On the main road. You'll see it—big sign saying Beauty Salon. Very nice-class place."

"This is very nice too. Here." I glanced round the caravan, not feeling a hypocrite, because in its own way it really was quite a little masterpiece. Doll looked pleased.

"Took a lump sum, instead of alimony. Bought the whole shenan, all at once."

Caught off guard, I blurted out, "Your divorce—it's through?"

"Sure. Six months ago. Just before I met you-know-who. Did he tell you we were waitin' for it?"

I stirred my coffee, feeling a flush of embarrassment. Doll leant over and patted my hand.

"That's OK, honey. I never told him I was a divorced lady. Men, they feel kinda freer if they think a girl's married—don't get so fearful of being tied down." She paused. "Mebbe I should have told him that first day he stopped in at the salon. Just wanted to use the phone, he said." The memory of their initial meeting softened her face, making it look suddenly younger. She got up briskly, started clearing away the plates, and added, with a show of cheerfulness,

"Some day, perhaps he'll say 'How's that divorce of yours comin' along, Doll?' And then I'll say, 'Why, Lover Boy, I'm free as a bird.' And then maybe he'll say, 'How about us getting married?' And then again, maybe he won't—you know how it is, with guys."

The Beauty Salon, which I passed half an hour later, turned out to be a small hut standing on an otherwise empty stretch of road, its windows bravely decked with coloured photographs of wanton-haired beauties. At the foot of a large shiny card, advertising Glide-on Lip Gloss, The Wettest Juiciest New Look For Lips were pencilled the words Free Coffee.

I must have been carried much further than I'd realised while I had dozed in the truck the night before, for the road soon started to go downhill, and remembering that Salt Lake City was about 3,000 feet lower than Rock Springs—4,000 feet above sea level, as against the plateau's 7,000—I got off for another ritual check of my bike.

It really was something of a farce, this business of checking Daisy, because I really hadn't the remotest idea of what to look for. I had brought along with me (with all its margins trimmed off to save weight) a paperback called *Bicycle Repairing for Beginners*, which guaranteed to bring bike maintenance down to a level that a child could understand.

I had tried studying *Bicycle Repairing* early on in the trip, so that if I broke down I would (hopefully) know what to do, but a few evenings of wrestling with such instructions as "using your third hand, slip the barrel end of your short transverse cable out of its curved prongs," and "if you have a blip or a blip and a wobble, take care of the blip first," I decided that it would be far better just to wait for the breakdown, and then try to learn how to fix it. After all, I argued, people hardly ever practised walking with crutches before they went ski-ing.

The net result was that I understood very little of the workings of my bicycle, and when I say I checked her over, what I really mean is that I just sort-of pawed her about, fiddling with things to see if they were noticeably looser or tighter than they had been the last time I had looked, and if I found that something had actually fallen off I would replace it from the little bag of odds and ends that Daisy's inventor had given me. I was far from sure where these goodies were really meant to go, so I worked on the principle of "if the cap fits, wear it," and twiddled them on wherever they looked happy.

My one great fear was that I would have a puncture. I hadn't mended one since I was nine years old, at which age I had had an elder brother to direct operations, and I wasn't at all confident that—even with the help of the things like bent teaspoons, marked Tyre Lifts—I would be able to get a tyre off.

And even if I did get it off, how would I ever get it back on again? Mercifully, I hadn't yet had a puncture; apart from signs of overall wear, the tyres, as I started the long descent to the Great Salt Lake, seemed in remarkably good shape.

Down, down went the road, winding through desolate scrublands backed by the inevitable barriers of snow-capped mountains.

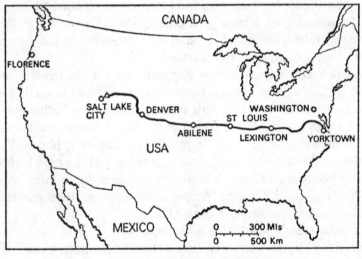

SALT LAKE CITY, UTAH

In 1847, when the Mormons had left the comparative safety of the Missouri plains to travel west in search of an "abiding place for the Saints," the plateau that I was just leaving had been a dangerous place and, to add to their problems, their leader Brigham Young had fallen ill while crossing it. When the travellers arrived at the glistening Salt Lake valley, he is said to have looked up from his portable sick-bed and said, "This is the place."

Considering that a contemporary writer described the valley as "a paradise of the lizard, the cricket and the rattlesnake," Brigham Young's enthusiasm seems a bit surprising—indeed, in those days, the valley must have looked every bit as arid as the country he had just crossed. Perhaps the poor man was just fed up with travelling; perhaps, though, he had a premonition of how the place would look a century later, for coming on it as I did—without any knowledge of what I was going to see—I found it breathtaking.

Below me lay a vast plain, almost completely covered by the buildings of an enormous city. Bounded on three sides by an immense barrier of snow-covered mountains, the fourth side of the plain—opposite to the pass by which I was entering—was lost in the misty outlines of a lake so apparently boundless that it might have been the sea. Early explorers had, indeed, thought it was the Pacific; only after they had laboriously circled it did they sadly admit that it was land-locked and, strangely, possessed no draining river. All the water that poured into it escaped by evaporation, which accounted for its saltiness.

At the centre of the huge city rose a complex of sky-scrapers, among which—dwarfed by its tall neighbours—squatted the six-towered Mormon temple, giving the impression more of having been conjured up by a medieval magician than designed by a nineteenth-century zealot. Brigham Young had decreed that the avenues of his new city should be wide enough to turn a four-oxen cart in; through these spacious streets I coasted towards the centre of the city feeling, on little Daisy, much as I had felt when as a child I once roller-skated down the Mall.

Surprisingly—after the chill of the high lands—the weather was again hot; I longed for a bath, and finding myself a hotel room lay soaking in some of the 400—against the national average of 50—gallons of water that each inhabitant of the city is said to use on every summer day. Wrapped in a big white bath-towel, I leant out of my fourteenth-floor window; from that vantage-point there seemed to be so much to see that I thought I'd spend two—or possibly even three—days in Salt Lake City. But first of all I'd go to the Visitors' Centre, to get a general idea of what went on.

The avenues in the middle of the city were planted with blos-

soming trees and edged with flower beds as colourful as English
herbaceous borders, but they had about them something of the
unnatural precision of the streets of a fictional space colony, so
that had someone told me that the arc above me was not true
sky but a plastic canopy separating me from interplanetary vacuum I wouldn't have been much surprised. Conversely, the roof
of the indoor shopping complex where I went to buy food was
so high, and so brightly lit, that it seemed more like true sky
than the glass that it really was; I had to go outside to re-check
what I remembered but couldn't believe—that above the shopping area rose thirty stories of concrete and steel.

Already a sense of unreality was beginning to creep up on me,
but for the moment it was chased away by the discovery, in a
health-food shop, of the first bit of good plain cheese that I had
seen since I had left home. I had never grown to like the American processed variety, which seemed to me to have the consistency of a bit of soap that's got lost in the bottom of a bath; I
sat on a park bench, munching happily on the cheese, and gazed
at a bronze group of a pioneer family, complete with their hand-
cart.

The cart had shafts, but a bar joined the front ends of these,
and where one might have expected to see a horse the figure of a
man was placed, leaning his weight against the bar as he hauled
with both hands on the shafts. Beside him stood his bonneted
wife; crowning the meagre household goods on the cart was a little girl, while a scarcely-bigger boy pushed at the hand-cart from
behind. Two thousand miles the pioneers had hauled those
hand-carts; it was strange to think how few life-spans separated
their pack-animal labours from the affluence of the present-day
population—my own grandfather, for instance, would have been
the right age to act as a model for the figure of the boy behind
the cart.

I dusted my fingers free of cheese-crumbs, and went into the
Visitors' Centre.

"Would you care for a guide?"

"No, thank you—I'm just looking around."

"May I explain our beliefs to you?"

"No, thanks. Perhaps later."

"Possibly you'd like to study some of these pamphlets?"

"How kind. But perhaps I'll just pick up some on my way out."

"Could I interest you in joining a tour of the Centre?"

"No, thank you—I'm quite happy on my own."

"Do take a seat. And what, especially, would you like to know about the Church of Jesus Christ of Latter-Day Saints? That's our real name, you know—'Mormon' is a sort of nick-name."

I gave in, and found myself shepherded into a sort of pen in the hall of the Visitors' Centre by a very neat, earnest man in a quite outstandingly well-ironed shirt.

Upstairs in the Centre, an enormous white statue of Christ dominated a vast circular hall painted to look like space, with the earth, moon and stars—ludicrously out of proportion—circulating among swirls of meringue-like clouds; around the perimeter of the hall groups of tourists sat in respectful silence, like hospital patients awaiting the arrival of a consultant. In an adjoining gallery, more tourists gazed reverently at a series of very large oil paintings depicting scenes from the life of Christ; a guide was declaiming proudly that there were 140 feet of paintings, which he described as a mural. Christ, as might be expected, was wearing a spotless white night-dress and the faces of the disciples appeared to have been copied from one of those nineteenth-century aldermanic group portraits that one comes across in provincial town halls.

I hurried into the next room, and found myself face-to-face with a huge piece of plate glass, behind which a plaster figure of a small boy knelt devoutly among some plastic fallen leaves in a top-lit imitation forest; a different guide explained to yet another reverent audience that "this beautiful three-dimensional diorama recreates the Sacred Grove where the young boy Joseph Smith had the Divine visitation which brought about the restoring of the Gospel to the earth." The moment of the Divine visitation was represented by a gradual brightening of the

light that fell on the upturned plaster face of the kneeling boy;
obliquely, the increased light also illuminated a notice that said
THE LIGHTING EFFECTS OF THIS SACRED DI-
ORAMA ARE ONLY TO BE ACTIVATED BY A
REGISTERED GUIDE.

Downstairs in the basement two cinemas were rapidly filling
with yet more tourists; the cinemas seemed identical, so I went
into the one that happened to be nearest, which was as luxurious as the most expensive in London—indeed, the whole Centre
was built with an obvious disregard for cost. Yet another well-
dressed young guide stood up in front of the screen, scanned the
auditorium to see that it was full and then, taking a key from his
pocket, unlocked a hatch by the entrance door and turned a
switch. Instantly, the doors of the auditorium slammed shut. It
was as if the gates of a prison had been locked behind me.

What was the film about? I can't remember, because I was so
disturbed by the idea of being locked in; but I do remember that
at the end the screen rose, revealing yet another three-dimensional diorama, this time made up of plaster shop-window children gazing as if mesmerised at an ever-brightening light, which
after a moment revealed yet another plaster model of Christ. A
stentorian voice intoned some religious platitude, curtains closed
in reverent silence over the scene, the door was electronically
opened and—oh, the relief of it—I was out again in the evening
sunshine.

The gardens around the Centre were full of couples taking an
evening stroll. Young husbands and wives, trailing assorted children; elderly couples walking slowly, arm in arm; teenage lovers
strolling decorously, not even touching hands; everyone seemed
to be with someone else, and everyone—but everyone—looked
well-dressed and quite amazingly the same. It was as if an ideal
couple had, at each stage of its development, been cloned to
reproduce a sufficient quantity of each age-group to acceptably
decorate the scene.

And now that I studied them more closely, even the flowers
were abnormally perfect—there didn't seem to be a fading

bloom among the pink-and-white, tighly-packed clusters that
lined the edges of the walkways. Again, I was overcome with the
scary feeling that I had somehow been transported into a
science-fiction world, where everyone and everything was plastic
and faultless and where nobody ever, ever did anything even remotely wrong. Such as have a drink, for instance.

I had read enough about the Mormons to know that they
eschewed all stimulants—not only alcohol, but tea, coffee and
even (because it contains a small amount of caffeine) Coke. Salt
Lake City is, however, no longer a "dry" town—one can buy
drinks if one wants to—but one of the very few rules I tried to
stick to was the one about "When in Rome, do as the Romans
do," and I felt reluctant, in a city where drinking is contrary to
religious beliefs, to walk into a shop and ask for a can of beer. So
I stomped back to my hotel, feeling very hot and—after the experience of the Visitors' Centre—badly in need of revival.

To cool down, I went out on to the balcony of my room
and there—tucked round a corner—was a demijohn of Californian rosé. How sad the previous occupants of the room must
have felt when they realised that they had left it behind. I
collected ice from the ice-making machine that stood in the corridor; then I unfolded the corkscrew part of my Boy Scout knife.
The evening sky outside my vertiginous window was so utterly
cloudless that the sun, as it sank, was visible as a complete incandescent circle, radiating orange beams in the manner of a
Christmas-card star of Bethlehem. Below, the enormous sprawl
of the city grew first invisible, then sprang back into view in the
form of an intricate web of lights. The mountains that ringed
the horizon turned mauve, then purple, and finally black.

The more I saw of Salt Lake City the next day, the more pro-
voked I found myself becoming by its smugness. Leaving aside
the fact that, in spite of it having been outlawed in 1890, some
25,000 Mormons were still believed to be practising polygamy—
which makes something of a nonsense of their bans on such
things as teenagers holding hands—I felt outraged to discover
that (at that time) the blacks in Utah still had to live in the

shadow of a Mormon dogma that declared them to be the "cursed sons of Cain" and officially denied them any hope of admission to the "celestial kingdom" after death.

Fuming at this and other discoveries, I took a tourist bus to visit what was advertised as "the biggest open-cast copper mine in the world"; I thought the trip might give me time to simmer down.

It wasn't only mentally that the bus trip lowered my temperature. Physically, it also froze me to the bone—for it was an air-conditioned bus, and the Americans seem to have a habit, when air-conditioning anything, of making the atmosphere far too cold for anyone wearing summer clothes. The same, of course, applies in reverse—their central heating almost roasts any European rash enough to wear "normal" European winter clothes.

The copper mine, some miles outside the city, was indeed fantastically big, the full-sized ore trains that circled the vast cavity seeming, when viewed from my observation hut on the rim of the mine, no larger than wire-worms. I leant on the guard-rail, watching men work half a mile below me.

"Excuse. Please, tell me what that indicates?"

I turned at the sound of the unfamiliar accent, expecting to have to deal with some completely unanswerable question about copper-mining. But the neatly dressed, bespectacled old man who had been standing behind me was pointing to the sign on a near-by vending machine.

The sign read SIX-FLAVORED MUSH. I considered it carefully. Soft drinks? Ice cream? And did whatever it was have six flavours all at the same time, or would one be expected to select one's preferred choice? It didn't take very long to come to a decision.

"It means," I said firmly, "nasty."

The old man didn't have a very fluent command of English. "Nass-ty?"

I clutched my stomach and made as if to vomit. "Bad for you. Disgusting. Ugh."

Light dawned. "Nass-ty. Ho ho. Ha-ha-ha." Giggling companionably, we clambered back into the sub-zero bus, on the way back to the city discovering that we were both travelling alone. He was, he told me, a Polish professor of geography, and feeling that elderly Polish professors probably don't go around propositioning strange women, I decided that the next move was up to me. Greatly daring, I suggested to the nice old man that we should have dinner together.

"I am very sorry, Madam—I must work. I stay here only a short time."

I was intrigued.

"I research," he replied to my question. "My family, we lose many records in the war. I research my ancestors in the Mormon library."

A Pole, looking for information about his forefathers in Utah? It sounded extremely far-fetched.

"It is true, believe me. They have many, many documents. Come with me. I will show you."

He took me to the door of the Genealogical Society Library— housed, in the way of most Mormon foundations, in a building that seemed like a cross between the Kensington Natural History Museum and the New York headquarters of the Chase Manhattan Bank—and I hadn't been inside it for more than five minutes before I realised that there was probably more information about Poles inside those walls than there had ever been in Warsaw. And the same would have been true for the French, the Spanish, the Dutch . . . in fact for almost any nation that kept written records.

Imagine three complete floors of an enormous building, filled with 130,000 volumes of family trees, 900,000 catalogued rolls of microfilmed documents, and 6 million family group records. Add a consultation service, a research survey service, instructional aids, church records, archives, a computer file index, and goodness only knows what else. And that's the Genealogical Society Library in Salt Lake City.

Fascinated, I wandered from floor to floor, studying the earnest researchers. Silent, dedicated, they staggered about under the weight of ancient ledgers, or flipped microfilm enlargements on to television-like screens. Hunched over spread-out documents, they sat copying, copying, copying; had monks looked like this, I wondered, before Caxton liberated them from manual transcription of the holy word? Over all the crowded floors hung a totally joyless obsession with the past; in their hundreds the people searched and searched for facts about their ancestors, their expressions withdrawn, worried, totally absorbed.

Among that throng of frenetic ants I suddenly experienced an acute loss of identity. All those busy people knew who they were —they knew where they lived, and other people knew their names. But in America, I didn't live precisely anywhere, and nobody knew me—I could wander for ever through that huge forest of bookshelves and never encounter anyone who had ever seen me before, let alone anyone who would know my name. Disconcertingly, I felt like a ghost, slipping unseen through the throng of the living. Who was I? Where was I?

In almost a state of panic, I hurried to the British section of the library, and took down a reference book. Thank goodness, there I was on page 1055, tucked neatly between my parents and my children. But the edition was ten years old—how could I be sure that I was still alive and wasn't a ghost looking up, in an outdated reference book, a self that had already vanished from the earth? Outside the library windows, the Martian city hummed in sterilised sunshine. I had to get back to the real world just as soon as ever I could. Checking out of my hotel, I fled down the road.

At first, the highway on which I was making my getaway wound along the shores of the Great Salt Lake. Intrigued since childhood by the idea of floating effortlessly on its briny water, I had been hoping to swim in it, but the sight of people paddling several hundred yards from the shore warned me that I would probably have to wade out about a mile before I'd be out of my depth, so I gave up the idea and pedalled on, past emerald-green golf courses and immaculately cultivated fruit farms.

After about 40 miles the road, which had been taking me due

north, veered north-east; this was where I began to pay for having made the side trip to Utah, because, having come unnecessarily far south-west, I would now have to bicycle north-east approximately parallel to the road I had travelled a few days before, so as to get back roughly to original position.

Perhaps it was something to do with the way maps are printed —with north at the top of the page—that made me feel that bicycling north was harder than bicycling south; I had a sort of mental picture, when heading north, of climbing up a page, and roads leading north always seemed to have more uphill gradients than ones going south. Travelling, as I now was, almost due north, by the time I crossed the border into Idaho I was tired and hungry. I stopped at a roadside café, intent on eating an Idaho Baked Potato—an outsize tuber served, all over the States, with chives and sour cream—but either it was the wrong time of year or else the entire crop had already been shipped to the restaurants of the big cities, for all the café could offer under the name of a Baked Potato was an incredibly nauseating candy bar, made of a sort of chewed-up-and-spat-out mush of shredded coconut encased in over-sweet chocolate.

I was sitting at a plastic-topped table contemplating this gastronomic disaster and brooding on the daunting length of the journey that still lay ahead, when I realised that a blind girl who I had noticed on my way into the café was still standing where I had first seen her, just inside the door. Her guide dog was sitting beside her, panting; the two of them almost blocked the narrow space by the door, so that people entering or leaving had either to edge or push past them; mostly, they pushed.

I watched for a moment, thinking that the girl must be waiting for someone, but as nobody came I got up and went over.

"Hello. Anything I can do for you?"

She turned her head towards the sound of my voice. "Would you tell me where the telephone is?"

"There's a small table just by your right hand, with nobody sitting at it. The telephone's on the wall, on the far side of it."

She put out her hand, located the table, circled it, patted the wall, and found the telephone.

"Got change?"

"Yes thanks. I'll be all right now—they'll come and pick me up."

Goodness only knows how long she'd been waiting, only about two yards from that phone; her horizon ended at her fingertips—how could I allow myself to feel downhearted because mine was still so far distant? Humbled, I bicycled on.

The next town was Logan—curiously Swiss-like in spite of the width of its streets—its broad valley ringed with yet more alplike mountains and its surrounding farms dotted liberally with munching cows. After that, the road wound up into country that was more like Scotland, with brown newly-ploughed fields separated by wild, open valleys.

The second day out, I reached Pocatello where—as every devotee of A Star Is Born knows—Judy Garland was born in a trunk. I was intrigued by its curious underground houses, like basements with roofs laid directly on top of them with no house in between. Was it at times so cold—or so hot—here that people had to take refuge underground, like the troglodytes of the Sahara? Or were they just abnormally apprehensive of the bomb? I followed my usual tactics of dropping into a small store and asking questions while my bill was added up.

"Those houses? Let me see now—you had cheese; the red pack, wasn't it? And the crackers, and an apple. . . ."

"Two apples—I ate one already. You were going to tell me about those houses, down the road?"

"Oh yes. D'd you want that bacon, or was you just looking?"

"I'd like to take it. And the oranges."

My change was carefully counted out. "You mean them hope-to places?"

"I'm not sure what they're called. They're kind-of underground, mostly."

"Oh yes—them's the hope-to's. Folks built basements, and hoped to put up the rest of the house later. Didn't get around to it though. Not enough cash. Say, you must have eaten that other apple real fast—never so much as saw the core."

By the time the sun started to go down the next day I was in the middle of an Indian reservation. I had thought that Indians, when actually inside their reservations, lived in a rather old-time way, so I was a bit surprised when a nice-looking young man offered me a lift, for with his high cheek-bones, olive skin, and straight coal-black hair he was obviously Indian, yet his jeans and checked cloth jacket were identical to those worn by other young Americans and his pick-up truck was indistinguishable from the thousands I'd already seen across the States.

We drove on through the reservation, passing a lot of small farms; they had a rather sad look—their yards often littered with wheel-less bicycles, wrecked cars, or derelict farm machinery. Even the fields had about them an air of poverty, as if they had grown weary of the effort of producing crops and had resigned themselves to a slow decline into infertility. When the young man told me that he himself was a farmer, I didn't quite like to ask him whether or not he enjoyed his work, so I said, "What do you like doing best, when you're not busy on the farm?"

His eyes suddenly brightened. "Hunting. Hunting and fishing. There's no end of game, up in the mountains."

Beyond the dreary fields the mountains of the Caribou National Forest rose craggily along the horizon; on my map, between them and the road on which we were travelling the words Blackfoot Reservation were printed. I longed to ask the young man if he was a Blackfoot, but wasn't sure how such a direct question would be received; instead, I asked, "Do you need a permit to go hunting?"

He smiled and shrugged his shoulders. "We just go hunting. Nobody bothers us. Take a gun 'n a blanket 'n maybe a bite to eat, and just go. Weeks, sometimes."

I felt glad that civilisation hadn't entirely taken over.

"Any bears up there?"

"Sure. Bear, elk, moose, mule deer, bobcats, red foxes, mountain lions—you name it, I can find it. Just about everything on four feet, up there."

While he was talking he had turned off the road on to a bumpy track that led up to a small wooden house. Behind the house a couple of corrugated-iron farm buildings rose forlornly from the usual scattering of discarded junk. But behind the corrugated-iron buildings, standing in a corner of a roughly harrowed field, I was elated to see the tall, conical shape of a tepee.

"Care for a cup of coffee?"

"Thanks. I'd be glad." I was still staring at the tepee. "Do you ever use it—for camping or anything?"

His eyes followed my glance. "Naw. Keep it there for the tourists, mostly. Photos. All that crap." He spoke suddenly roughly, as if either ashamed or embarrassed.

Two girls rode up on small energetic ponies. They had the same glossy black hair as the young man and their legs gripped the bare flanks of the ponies with a sort of casual professionalism, as if riding was to them so natural an activity that they no longer gave it any conscious thought.

"Hi!" said the first girl, sliding off her pony and looping its rope halter-reins over the tail-gate bolt of the truck. Her short dress might have come out of any mail-order catalogue but her brown legs—insouciantly bared as she dismounted—had a sinewy look, like the legs of an over-trained dancer. "Don't anyone get to be introduced, round here?"

"My sisters," said the young man, rotating his wrist. "Sorry, but I've forgotten what you said your name was?"

The turn of phrase interested me. It wasn't "what your name was," but "what you *said* your name was"—a hang-over, perhaps, from the days when not all strangers wanted to disclose their identity. I gave the shortened version of my name, having discovered that my complete first name was one that, in America, was normally only given to boys.

"You stopping with us, Chris?" asked the second girl, as we sat drinking the coffee. I hadn't actually thought of it, but now that I did, the idea seemed appealing.

"I'd love to put my tent up somewhere, if you wouldn't mind."

"Sure, be our guest." She waved an expansive hand, taking in the major part of Idaho.

I found a spot close to the tepee, and started to tap in my tent's skewer-like pegs. The girls stood watching; the way that my tent blossomed out of its tiny bag always intrigued spectators—it was a sort of Instant Tent, springing from the size and shape of a rolled-up shirt to a neat little den by the simple addition of two telescopic poles and seven spider-thin guy-ropes. On a good day I could erect it in five minutes and take it down—if I wasn't too fussy about the way I rolled it—in even fewer.

"You going to use that for sleeping, Chris?"

"It's really very snug."

One girl faked a shudder. "I'd as soon sleep in there," she said, tilting her head in a derogatory sort of way towards the tepee, as if the idea of sleeping anywhere but in a house was faintly barbaric.

She had given me an idea. "Could I?" I asked.

"Could you what?"

"Sleep in the tepee?"

Both girls giggled uncontrollably. "Sure—if you was a fowl."

I heard only the sound of the word, and didn't grasp its meaning.

"A fowl—chicken—you know." They danced joyously round in a circle, fists in armpits and elbows flapping, miming an agitated hen. "The chickens, they roost there all winter. We only cleaned it out yesterday, ready for the tourists. Come and look inside, if you like—no charge to friends of the family."

Doubled up with laughter at their own jokiness, they unlaced the door. Inside, the tepee was surprisingly spacious. True, it still smelt quite strongly of its winter tenants, but the earth floor had been swept and the woven rugs that covered most of it looked completely new.

"Scuffle around on them a bit, would you?" said the older girl.

"Folks, they kinda think rugs is more genuine if they've had a bit of wear."

She ground one heel into a rug, and swung her body from side to side as if dancing.

"We get 'em wholesale," she confided. "Jes' put out a few at a time and sell 'em straight off the floor." She studied her own rotating foot, lifted it, and moved it to a fresh unmarked part of the rug. "Do you really want to sleep in here?" she asked again, incredulous.

Around midnight I woke and watched a bright, unknown constellation wheel slowly over the smoke-hole at the apex of the tepee. I stretched out a hand and ran it over the age-dried hide of the section behind my head. Where had this tepee been pitched in years gone by, I wondered? Had papooses been born in it, or feathered braves slept their last night on earth within its shelter, before the final massacre at Wounded Knee? The night air was very cold and still, and in the silence I thought for a moment I could hear a wolf howl. "Don't be silly," I told myself, "wolves have been extinct for decades around here. It's just a dog. Of course."

IDAHO, MONTANA AND WYOMING

An altimeter, I thought—that's what I really need. A compass, which of course I carried, was all right for checking that my map was the right way up, and for siting my tent so that it pointed towards the rising sun. But an altimeter would, at this point, have been really useful. On my journey from the east coast to the west, I wasn't making any very significant deviations either north or south, neither was I travelling for long enough for the seasons to play much of a part in the changes of temperature that I was experiencing; these were due almost entirely to changes in altitude, and lacking any reliable way of working out how high I was, the rapid swings from cold to hot—and back again to cold— were continually taking me by surprise. For instance, although I was now only a few days away from the oppressive heat of Salt Lake City, the weather had turned so cold that I had to bicycle with the hood of my anorak pulled up over my little orange hat, and as I left the little Idaho country town of Ashton I found a dead short-eared owl lying on the road, frozen so stiff that, picking it up to move it from the tarmac, I thought at first that it was carved from wood.

It had been a relief to spend a night in a motel at Ashton, because although I much appreciated the hospitality that people gave me it was sometimes quite exhausting, at the end of a long day of physical effort, to keep sociably on my toes. Just to flop down on a motel bed, television tuned to some undemanding programme, was restful not only to my muscles but also to my mind. Camping, of course, offered its own form of peace, but although—from a combination of fresh air and tiredness—I slept very soundly in my tent, during the hours that I was awake in it I never totally relaxed. In my tent, I was always slightly on the alert, whereas with the four walls of a motel cabin around me—and the door securely locked—I could really unwind.

This morning, after a good night's rest, I had started so early that the sun was still striking almost horizontally across the wild, desolate countryside. The ploughed fields that ringed Ashton had soon given way to tough, tussocky grasslands, backed by conifer forests which, climbing over rolling foothills, faded in the distance into mountains seamed and striped with snow. Far to the east—black against the red ball of the rising sun—the three pointed peaks of the Tetons stabbed at the sky.

Still heading north, I was by now at about the 44th line of latitude—the one that bisects Lake Michigan and then reaches out to Genoa, Belgrade and—rather surprisingly—Vladivostok—and climbing into the foothills, it seemed as if I would be bicycling for ever through dark forests. Sedge-bordered lakes with romantic names came and went, and, as if to show that the region wasn't as deserted as it appeared, a notice at the gate of a side-track threatened TRASPASSERS WILL BE SHOT AT ON SIGHT. TRY IT AND SEE. Other notices, less aggressive—and better spelt—warned of the possibility of meeting motorised snow-sledges—a reminder that I was lucky to be travelling in such an early spring, for in normal years most of this region would still have been under snow.

Around lunch-time I came on a roadside notice that said WELCOME TO MONTANA, under which was written, in smaller letters, CONTINENTAL DIVIDE, ELEVATION 7072. Ignorantly, I had imagined that each continent had only one continental divide—a sort of backbone from which rivers flowed in opposite directions—but although I had crossed one American continental divide on the top of the Rockies, here I was, quite clearly, crossing another. It was confusing.

The sun, shining brightly, lit the forests and lakes and mountains with the clarity of a Pre-Raphaelite painting, each distant
peak defined as precisely as the nearest pine-needle on the
closest tree. The air was cold, but the sun warmed my back, and
coasting downhill felt pleasantly like ski-ing—the same effortless
skim over the ground, the same crisp intake of breath, the same
feeling of total physical well-being. Pushing Daisy up hills was
slightly less pleasant, not only because it was hard work but also
because, travelling at only walking pace, I was distinctly worried
about bears.

Ever since Pocatello people had been telling me alarming stories about the bears. Because the spring was so early they had, it
seemed, come out of hibernation sooner than usual, and were
prowling about feeling very peckish at a time of year when their
normal food was not yet freely available. Nobody seemed entirely sure what they would be eating in a normal spring—
opinions varied from the downright repulsive (garbage, carrion
and insect larvae) through grass, berries, eggs and nuts to such
gourmet items as honey and salmon, but everyone was unani-
mous as to what constituted their really favourite delicacy—
tourist. Particularly female tourist—if I was to believe what I
was told, several of these were clawed out of their tents and
crunched up every year; the only reason, people whispered, that
this fact wasn't more widely known was that the authorities, so
as not to discourage holiday trade, found ways of keeping the
stories out of the press.

I had read in my animal reference book that the locality har-
boured not only black or cinnamon bears (*Ursus americanus*)
but also grizzlies, sub-titled (encouragingly) *Ursus horribilis*.
Ursus horribilis, the book said, could bulk up to 850 pounds
(more than four times the weight of a heavyweight boxer),
stand between 6 and 7 feet tall (presumably even more if on tip-
toes) and had curved claws up to 4 inches long. They preferred,
it seemed, to hunt in the twilight, but "might be abroad at any
time of day or night."

What, I asked, should I do if I was menaced by a bear? Fire

your gun into the air, I was advised—that's usually enough to scare them off. "But I haven't got a gun," I would answer. As usual, when I said this, everyone looked faintly shocked.

OK then, they would go on, rather despairingly—you'd best climb a tree. But be sure it's a thin tree—bears climb trees by embracing them with their paws, and don't like tackling ones that are so spindly that, so to speak, they shake hands with themselves around the trunk. I had a nasty vision of a thin tree, with me clinging to the top, bending gracefully over and delivering me straight into the jaws of Teddy, and any tree strong enough not to bend would, I suspected, be climbable by a bear of even moderate enthusiasm.

Where the land on each side of the road was fairly open I wasn't too worried, but when the trees crowded close I found myself looking anxiously for any large brownish-black objects that might be lurking in the shadowed depths of the forest. It was no good deluding myself that a passing motorist might, if necessary, leap out of his car and rescue me. To begin with, if I had been a passing motorist, and I'd seen a dirty great bear getting out its knife and fork, I know just what I would have done— I'd have kept on passing. And on top of that, there were hardly any vehicles on the road. Occasional lorries thundered by—the drivers tooting their horns in friendly greeting—and the odd pick-up truck hurried past on local business, but for most of the time there was no sound but the soughing of the breeze in the tops of the pine-trees and the faint hiss of my tyres on the tarmac. I wasn't entirely sorry when, at the end of what was one of the most dramatically beautiful rides of the trip, I found myself bicycling, stiff-kneed, into West Yellowstone.

I had got so used to American country towns having monotonously similar streets that West Yellowstone came as a considerable surprise. West Yellowstone was, to put it mildly, unlike any other town on earth. To begin with, it wasn't exactly a town, but more a collection of motels, petrol stations, restaurants and souvenir shops, scattered like brightly-coloured debris among a forest of tall pines. The trees, which somebody had had the forethought to leave standing, were the main charm of the town, which otherwise would have looked both garish and deserted, for, with only the permanent residents around, the whole place had an air of under-population.

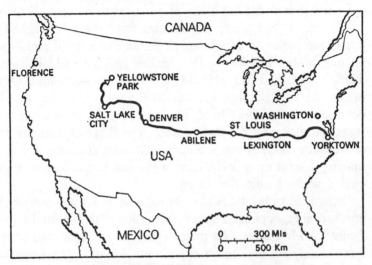

YELLOWSTONE PARK, WYOMING

"You should see it in summer," said the proprietor of the motel that I had picked haphazardly from among the dozens that lined the wide, unpaved roads. "Streets just solid with people—walking around, drinking, singing, having fun. Past midnight, every night. Yes, indeed, quite a place."

He filled a polystyrene bowl with frozen cubes, each one dimpled like a nymphet's navel.

"Ice?" he inquired, giving the bowl a nudge in my direction.

"Oh—thanks." I didn't really want ice but it seemed bad-mannered to refuse. "But doesn't everyone come here to see the geysers?"

"Sure. That's what they say. But I guess it's more like they just want an excuse to take a trip. Most folks, if they're stopping a couple of nights, they just drive in to see Old Faithful, and then they come right on out again. Rest of the time, it's drinking. Drinking and so on. You know."

He moved the ice-bowl another inch towards me, and glanced rather cynically out of the window. "Well, it's all trade, I guess. Shouldn't grumble."

I went to look for my room. It was at the end of a courtyard of identical rooms, each with its own front door, and held the usual twin beds and television set. There was a small metal box on one of the bedside tables, marked MAGIC MASSAGE— THE THRILL YOU MUSTN'T MISS. Smaller print urged me to put 25 cents into the slot on the top of the box and lie down on the bed next to it. Intrigued, I followed the instructions, and instantly the mattress began to shake as if in the grip of an earthquake. It was a sensation at once alarming and sickmaking; I leapt up quickly, leaving the bed to shudder on unoccupied while I unloaded Daisy.

Being able to bring Daisy right into my room was one of the great advantages of staying in motels, rather than normal hotels; I could nearly always get a room on the ground floor, and even if I could only get one on an upper level, I could carry Daisy upstairs and keep her in my bedroom overnight. There was virtually no service in motels but its absence was made up for by the freedom that I had to do as I pleased. Somehow I couldn't imagine that a hawk-eyed concierge would tolerate a guest taking a bicycle into a French hotel room, but in an American motel nobody ever even tried to stop me doing so, and having Daisy in my room not only assured her safety but also gave me a modicum of companionship.

Although I was meeting a great number of people, and so was never technically lonely, I was beginning to suffer slightly from the lack of continuity in my relationships—it was a case of new people, new people, new people all the time, and among these ever-changing relationships the permanence of my alliance with Daisy was beginning to take on considerable importance to me. To see her waiting for me in my room when I got back from dining out in a strange town was like being welcomed home by a faithful dog; I never actually got to the point of talking to her, but I did develop a sort of dependence on her company, and if I had lost her I think I would have been extremely upset.

Tonight, feeling very hungry, I decided to stand myself a really good meal; I got myself a table at what was said to be the best restaurant in town and was amazed, for about the twentieth time, by the amount that Americans spent on eating out.

It was the sort of restaurant that, in England, couples would only go to for some sort of celebration, such as an anniversary, but here in America men were quite obviously taking out their entire families—including the children—and treating the meal as something quite everyday. The phenomena couldn't be explained by a difference in the price of food, which I was finding if anything cheaper than in England—it could only be explained by the difference in the amount of spending-money that the Americans, as opposed to the English, kept after they had paid their taxes. For the people tucking into the sea-food and steaks around me weren't particularly rich Americans—they were the year-round inhabitants of a country town; I couldn't help thinking how nice it would be if the average Englishman could afford to take his family out in the same way.

The next morning, suitably terrified by yet more bear horror stories, I bicycled off into Yellowstone Park. The road inside the park gates was completely deserted; it ran through a towering forest of pines, and during the first twenty minutes I saw fifteen ravenous bears, which I thought must be something of a record. It wasn't until, almost petrified with fear, I'd cleared the forest and got out into open geyser country that I felt sane enough to admit that what I'd seen hadn't been bears, but rotting tree-stumps.

The amount of both these black-brown stumps and of tangles of fallen trees had been something I hadn't expected. In England, all forests are at least marginally manicured and, never having seen a forest where dead trees are allowed to lie exactly where they fall, I had no idea of how chaotic and prehistoric-looking such a wild forest could be.

It is, in fact, only the areas designated as "wilderness" that the Americans leave entirely to the whims of nature—their "national" forests are cared for much like English ones—but I found the wilderness ones quite frightening. I had the feeling that if I ever lost my way in one of them, I would be so exhausted by the effort of clambering over the spillikin-puzzle of fallen trees that I would never get out.

I had been looking forward to Yellowstone Park, but as usual, I had got quite the wrong idea about it. Travelogue films had led me to think that it would be about the size of an English park—easily explored in an afternoon—and that there would be lots of friendly rangers to direct me to the one-and-only geyser, Old Faithful.

But it wasn't the size of an English park—it was enormous; 2,248,120 acres, or getting on for the same size as Kent, Sussex and Surrey combined. What's more, there were no rangers around—it seemed they were taking their pre-season holiday— and as for Old Faithful being the only geyser, there were over ten thousand of them, if one counted in the thermal springs and pools.

The wonders of the Yellowstone region were hardly even guessed at by the early settlers until 1805, when the governor of the Louisiana Territory sent an Indian map to President Jefferson, showing "a volcano on the Yellowstone River." Since then, it has become one of the biggest tourist attractions in the world; now, in the out-of-season spring, the park was almost deserted, but during the summer cars and caravans sometimes fill its roads almost bumper to bumper, and the rangers have to use walkietalkies to clear "bear jams"—traffic snarls caused by motorists pulling up to watch the bears.

I got ready to take a photograph of Daisy silhouetted against Old Faithful; except for a couple with a small baby—cocooned papoose-like in a nylon sling—I was alone in the huge circle of benches that, in the holiday season, would hold hundreds of sight-seers patiently waiting for each hourly eruption. I felt sure that this would be the only chance that a little English folding bicycle would have of holding the stage in front of that impressive backdrop, and I was determined to make the photograph a good one. But the young couple were feeling both friendly and curious; Daisy intrigued them.

"Would you mind showing it to Junior? I'm sure he'd be real interested."

From the snug security of its mother's back, the baby gazed blankly at me, pinkish eyelids dropping over sky-blue irises. I felt a bit nonplussed.

"Of course . . . if you like. But I'm not sure he'll really. . . ."

"Oh yes—he's a very receptive child. Highly alert to new experiences. That's why we take him everywhere with us. The first year is so very important."

She turned slightly, presenting her back—with the baby on it —to me. One minuscule mittened fist was withdrawn from the confines of the sling and stuffed into a mouth as small and wet as a newly-opened oyster. Drugged by the delectable flavour of washed wool, the baby sagged forward, tumbled his head on his mother's spine, and closed his eyes.

"Is he looking at your bicycle? Perhaps if you held it up, nearer his face?"

"I think he's . . . well, perhaps he's dozing a little."

"Oh, but he couldn't be. He's going to watch Old Faithful." She craned her head round, trying to look down her own back. "Hey, Marvin!" Her husband, who was adjusting his camera at the edge of the boardwalk that surrounded the geyser, glanced up anxiously and hurried back to her side. "Marv, I think Junior's dropped off."

For a fleeting moment the father's face expressed all the concern of a man who, misinterpreting a sentence, believes that his child has undergone a possibly damaging fall. He checked the safety of the baby, who was now obviously fast asleep, and gazed earnestly at its tiny crumpled face.

"I think he's taking a little nap," he announced sagaciously.

"But what shall we do?" wailed the girl. "All this way, and

he's going to miss Old Faithful. And we can't wait for the next eruption—it'll be a half-hour after his feed time."

"Try jumping up and down."

"I'm just not strong enough yet, Marv. You just don't realise what giving birth does to your stomach muscles. You take him, if you're so set on waking him."

With a noise that was a cross between an old-fashioned steam train and a fully-opened bath tap the giant geyser suddenly started to erupt, spouting steam and boiling water nearly 200 feet into the air.

"Oh, it's too late, it's too late," the girl cried, ceasing her attempt to free her shoulders from the sling. As I raised my camera, I had a sideways impression of her husband clasping her round the waist and vigorously bouncing her up and down, while the baby—who all this activity was presumably supposed to wake—flopped on her back in a continued state of oblivion.

I bicycled off, skirting geysers shaped like castles or grottos, punch-bowls or fountains or dragons' mouths, past prismatic pools coloured emerald green or orange or scarlet or morning-glory blue. Enormous bison, said to weigh about 2,000 pounds—about the same as an average family car—roamed upland pastures with slow, dignified confidence; I didn't dare go close to photograph them, having heard they could charge at 40 miles an hour—more than twice as fast as a sprinting man.

The elk, moose and mule deer, browsing tranquilly in meadows bordered by tumbling streams, didn't scare me and—which was even more important—I didn't scare them, so I could photograph them from very near, as I could the Canada geese, a breed that is usually so shy that they post sentries when they feed. As, beside a lake, I snapped away at the geese, an osprey hawked over the reeds where they were feeding, hovered for a moment on beating wings, then plunged feet-first into the lake, rising again almost instantly with a fish in its talons. As it made off with its strange crook-winged flight, the drops of water clinging to its feathers gave it the appearance of being spangled with diamonds.

Further on in the park, a vast terracotta-red gorge captured and then released—in an immense white waterfall—a river which would, hundreds of miles to the west, eventually join the Mississippi. I crossed another pass marked Continental Divide; the elevation was over 8,000 feet and the road was edged with snow drifts. An hour later I had coasted down to thermal springs marked with signs warning that their temperature was dangerously hot.

But much as I would have liked to, I couldn't linger, and two days later I was again heading north, on a forty-mile stretch of road that snaked between the Beaverhead and the Gallatin National Forests, both of which had the beauty that I had expected —and not found—in the main part of the Rockies. The valley down which I was travelling was quite narrow, dotted by widely separated ranches. Some of these were of the "dude" type, providing a painless taste of outdoor life for holidaymakers; horses stood about in wooden-fenced fields, resting in preparation for their arduous summer task of carrying unskilled riders. Behind the ranches, forests and foothills soared upwards towards towering snow-capped mountains.

At a turn-off that led to a ski resort I stopped at a roadside café; it was obviously geared to cope with crowds of skiers, but now I was the only customer.

"It's that crazy thaw," confided the girl behind the counter, busying herself with toasting my sandwich. I would have been just as happy to have it untoasted, but she seemed keen to have something to do. "Not a flake of snow left. Makes you cry."

A bell rang on the microwave oven; she opened it and took out my sandwich, which had miraculously turned golden inside a paper bag. "Ketchup?"

I shook my head. "What do you do, after the thaw? Most years?"

"Oh, this place stays open—twelve months. I could just stick around. But usually, I get myself a summer job on one of the dude places. Makes a change. Change of company, too."

She giggled, her pigtailed hair bouncing on her pert T-shirted bosom.

"Have you always worked here, since you left. . . ." I was going to say "school" but changed it to "college?" The slightly surprised reaction of Americans when they learnt that I myself had never been to college had made me realise that not to be a "college girl" could be interpreted as being pretty low down on the social scale, so now I always played for safety and assumed that acquaintances had continued their education beyond high-school level.

She scooped some crushed ice into a paper beaker, and helped herself to a Coke. "Naw. Used to have a job in the park. That was real fun, except for the peke ladies."

I bit into the hot cheese of my sandwich, and looked inquiring.

"Peke ladies—old biddies with rhinestone glasses, crazy little dogs on fancy leads. Air-conditioned mobile homes, wrinkly knees. Passed remarks if my shirt wasn't buttoned up fit to strangle me. Jealous. As if I'd want to give the time of day to one of their old guys. Silly cows."

"Is that what made you . . . er . . . decide to leave?"

"Naw. Not really. I got busted too often. Hot-potting."

A small, glutinous globule of melted Cheddar detached itself from the corner of my sandwich and fell on the plastic counter-top; the girl pulled a paper napkin from a chrome holder and, with an absent-minded air, wiped the counter. It didn't look as if she was going to say any more, so I prompted.

"Hot-potting? Tell me?"

"In the slack season. Nothing to do. Well, that is, not unless you're going steady. Then—oh well, you know. But if you're not crazy about someone, or into drugs or something, it's just dead boring, up at Yellowstone. So some of us, we'd go hot-potting—swimming in the hot springs at night."

I remembered the thermal springs, apparently bubbling up from the very core of the earth, and felt quite scared at even the idea of diving into one of them. The dismay must have showed on my face, for the girl laughed.

"Rangers don't like it, either—give us breakfast in Mammoth if they catch us." (Mammoth was the name of a town at the north entrance of the park.) "Breakfast in Mammoth, that means they slap us in jail for the night, and call our folks to come and fetch us out next morning."

I rode clear of the mountains, and coasted into a town called Bozeman. I felt a bit ashamed that I knew nothing whatever about Bozeman. But then, I knew nothing about an awful lot of American towns. The sheer size of the country—I was still, because of the side-trip I made to Salt Lake City, only about three-quarters of the way across it—and the almost unimaginable number of its towns and villages was really beginning to confuse me.

All my life, the geographical United States had appeared in my mind's eye as little more than a particularly orderly map. There had been a lot of conveniently easy-to-draw straight-line boundaries, some blue bits at the top (the Lakes), a white strip on the left (the Rockies) and about ten important cities (marked with dots), and I had never consciously realised—until I started my bicycle trip—that nearly all the blank spaces on my mental map held a large number of towns, most of which had clearly been around for a long time and all of which would have been justifiably insulted if a dusty stranger on a bicycle had admitted that, right up to the time when she crossed the town limits, she had never heard of them.

I decided that I would really make an effort to get to know this next town; unfortunately, I arrived there only an hour ahead of a tornado.

WYOMING, MONTANA AND IDAHO

There was a historical museum at the University of Bozeman, and I was bicycling to the campus to pay it a visit; on the way, I unpacked my lunch in a mini-park, beside an otherwise bleak street. I much enjoyed this park, which—although it only measured a few yards in each direction—boasted a bench, two courageous saplings, and a small Japanese-type bridge crossing a make-believe stream (make-believe because the channel beneath, although painted a cheerful blue, was completely dry). There was also an entrance arch that, liberally encrusted with fragments of broken china, would have looked quite at home outside Bangkok's Wat Arun—the Monastery of Dawn. The whole tiny oasis was roofed, as if by a rainbow, with an almost tangible aura of loving care, and I felt happier just from having picnicked in it.

But when I remounted Daisy, the wind, which before my picnic had only raised little swirls of dust in the gutters, had grown so strong that I had difficulty in pedalling against it, and by the time I reached the campus the air was hitting me—now on one side, now on the other—as if I had been a boxer's punching-ball.

Across the spacious acres of the university's playing-fields I glimpsed athletes hastily grabbing sweaters and racing for shelter, and as I bent to secure Daisy to the railings by the museum steps the wind, grabbing my hair by the roots, slicked it into a horizontal streamer that cracked like a cattle-herdsman's whip.

Fighting every inch of the way, I reeled up the steps of the museum and leant against the heavy wooden door. It didn't budge. Hastily, I looked round for a bell; there wasn't one. I threw myself against the solid panels, and this time the door miraculously opened, and I fell rather than walked inside.

As the massive doors swung shut behind me, it was as if someone had lifted the needle from an over-noisy gramophone record. The roar of the wind vanished, and was replaced by a faint click-click. I looked around, and saw that the sound came from the rapidly-moving knitting-needles of a bright-eyed middle-aged lady, sitting behind a desk on which stood a sign saying INFORMATION.

She smiled welcomingly. "Quite a storm out there?"

"Yes indeed. Do you often get them?"

"Well, sometimes we do, and sometimes we don't."

She had a kind face, which made up for the vagueness of her answer, so I smiled back and wandered off into the main hall of the museum.

Quite the most interesting thing about museums, I think, is not so much what is in them as what people have thought worth putting in them. For instance, the museum at Bozeman had one exhibit consisting of no less than 275 different kinds of barbed wire. I absolutely could not drum up much interest in short lengths of wire, but what was fascinating was to stand in front of that bizarre display and ponder on why some learned curator had felt that barbed wire was so germane to the ethos of Bozeman.

Visions of land claims and cattle-rustling and shoot-outs round water-holes sprang to life; railway engines puffed—hooting mournfully—down lines so newly-laid that the cuttings had not yet sprouted grass; isolated homesteads sent thin pennants of chimney-smoke into skies that until only a few seasons before had known only the grey plumes of camp fires. In those pioneer days, the difference in the twist of lengths of barbed wire, which was going to define the prairie farmer's private property and so

revolutionise the entire life-style of the west, must have been of
vital importance.

I felt I had learnt something fundamental about Bozeman,
not because someone had been industrious enough to assemble
and mount all those scraps of wire, but because someone, knowing infinitely more than I did about the history of the locality,
had felt that such an action was worth doing.

The museum was full of other interesting relics, including a
saddle with a sort of open valley down the middle in place of
that hard ridge that normally tries to saw novice riders in half.
But although the saddle, and the town's first fire engine, and
the reproduction of an Early Settler's Home were all very nice,
after a while I felt I'd better be getting on. I went to the entrance.

It was as if I'd inadvertently opened the door of a tiger's cage,
and the beast had sprung on me. I staggered back, fighting to
shut the heavy panels.

"Still blowin'?" inquired the lady behind the desk. A ball of
baby-blue wool popped out of the pocket of her cardigan and
rolled, as if in a state of perpetual motion, down the long corridor that lay behind her. "Oh my ears and whiskers," said the
lady mildly, turning her head to watch it go.

I strolled back into the museum, resigned to the prospect of
spending more time there, but after I'd had another look at the
barbed wire, and the fire engine, and the Early Settler's Home, I
suddenly began to feel extremely sleepy. All I wanted was a
quiet corner where I wouldn't disturb anyone if I just happened
to snore. And of course, I couldn't find one.

In desperation, I pushed open the door of the restroom, but,
unless I'd draped myself along the taps, it had no place for me to
sleep. Then I tried a few of the chairs in the main hall, but I felt
pretty sure that if I dropped off—metaphorically speaking—in
one of them, I'd drop off literally as well. Next, I toyed with the
idea of reclining in the rocking chair in the Early Settler's
Home, but the management had evidently heard about vandals
like me, and had tied a bit of string from one cherrywood arm to

the other, adding, for good measure, a notice saying EXHIBI-
TION PURPOSES ONLY.

By now I was getting absolutely dizzy with sleep. I wondered
if I could snooze standing up, like a horse. Then suddenly I
spotted the ideal place—the Model T Ford. This venerable car
was, as befitted its place in history, raised on a sort of platform,
so that the actual seats were not visible to anyone standing at
floor level. Glancing around with all the furtiveness of a poten-
tial shop-lifter, I checked that I was alone in the main hall; then
I opened the car door, clambered up, and shut myself inside. A
brief wriggle to find the most comfortable position, and I was
away in the land of nod.

I don't know how long I slept, but suddenly I awoke with the
impression that I was in a school playground. The air was filled
with excited childish cries and the slither and stomp of infant
feet. Cautiously, I raised my head and squinted over the side of
the car; the entire floor below me was alive with children.

Small boys shoved other small boys; small girls pulled each
other's hair or stuck fingers into each other's eyes; little boys
looked anxiously around for somewhere to pee and little girls,
not bothering, happily wet their knickers. It was, in fact, a typi-
cal School Educational Outing, and my heart went out to whatever luckless teacher was in charge. It also went out a bit to myself, because I realised that I would have to stay in the Model T
until they all cleared off.

But hardly had I made the decision to lie low when I heard a
scrabbling noise; urchin feet were quite clearly trying to gain a
purchase on the Ford's high running-board, and a second later
the crew-cut head of a male tot rose slowly over the side of the
car. Wide-open eyes gazed at me with amazement, then, with a
cry that mingled fright with surprise, the boy let go his grip and
dropped back on to the floor of the museum.

"Hey, Miss! Miss! There's a woman in there—in that old
car!"

The voice of the teacher rose calmingly above the general
chatter.

"Nonsense, dear. There can't possibly be. And how many times have I got to tell you not to climb on the exhibits?"

"But there is! There is! And she's *dead*."

At the word "dead" a hush fell over the children. Although from my slouched-down position I couldn't see them, I could sense them gathering round the platform; the idea of seeing a real dead body held, it was obvious, considerable appeal.

"Go on, Miss—have a look. I bet she's been dead for years and years. Hundreds of years—ever since that crummy car got wrecked."

"It's not wrecked, dear—that's the way cars used to look, in olden days."

The teacher must have been a tallish girl. I could just see the top of her beret over the side of the car; it had a sort of pom-pom on it, and I had a sudden wild urge to bounce up like a jack-in-the-box and bop it with my bag. But then I saw the handle of the car door turn, and a second later I was gazing eyeball-to-eyeball into the earnest, spectacled face of what must surely have been one of the most surprised young women in Montana. It was a small door—it was a small car—and standing directly in front of it, she effectively blocked all view of me from the children. A true Daughter of the Revolution, she came to a lightning decision; even as she gazed at me—with all the glad enthusiasm of a hostess finding a mouse in the mayonnaise—she was speaking reassuringly over her shoulder.

"What nonsense you do talk, dear. Why, of course there's nobody in here. Now run along, children, there's lots to see over on the other side of the hall."

And she shut the door firmly, as if to convince herself—as effectively as she had her charges—that the car was empty.

The next sizeable town after Bozeman, as I headed west, was Butte, Montana, where I arrived late one evening after a trip of about a hundred miles over flattish farming country outlined by yet more alp-like mountains. The weather had turned cold and rainy, making the journey seem about twice as long as it really was, and perhaps also accounting for the rather jaundiced view

I took of Butte, which is no doubt an elysian town, much loved by its native sons, but which seemed to me both chilly and lacking in architectural charm.

By now, anyway, I was much looking forward to getting to Missoula, which housed the headquarters of a bicycling organisation whose officials had given me a lot of encouragement; they had even sent me maps without asking for payment in advance—a type of trustful generosity rare among map-suppliers. These nice people housed and fed me in Missoula, and sent me on my way with delightful sketches of the places where I should camp on the next stretch of my journey; this would be down the Lochsa river, which actually flowed towards the Pacific.

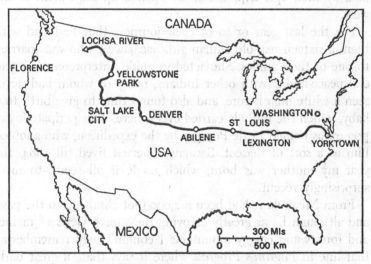

LOCHSA RIVER, IDAHO

Standing at the top of a pass in the range of mountains that separates Montana and Idaho, I looked at this westward-flowing river and for the first time really believed that I was going to get to the Pacific, for wasn't I on the route of those intrepid explorers, Lewis and Clark?

Lewis was the man to whom Thomas Jefferson, the President

of the United States from 1801 to 1809, gave the job of finding out if there was a useable water route across the continent. Lewis, by profession a soldier, invited Clark, who had also been in the army but who had since become a farmer, to join him, and in 1804 the expedition set out from St. Louis to look for the source of the Missouri—the river that, flowing eastwards, joins the south-flowing Mississippi at St. Louis.

Eighteen months later, after many adventures in some of the wildest and most spectacular terrain of North America, they travelled down the westward-flowing Columbia river to the Pacific. Unfortunately, when they got back to St. Louis in 1806, they had to report that there was no direct waterway, but they had, by their epic trip, effectively opened up huge areas of the west.

For the last year or so of their journey, they had had with them a sixteen-year-old Indian girl, Sacajawea, who was married to one of their guides. She acted as guide, interpreter, and general peace-maker with other Indians, many of whom had never seen a white man before, and also found time to give birth to a baby, which she blithely carried everywhere. This peripatetic papoose was named Little Pompey by the expedition, who adopted him as a sort of mascot. Sacajawea herself lived till 1884, the year my mother was born, which made it all seem—to me—surprisingly recent.

From Missoula it had been a 2,000-foot climb up to the pass, and although I was greatly enjoying the superb views of ravines and forests and craggy mountains I couldn't help remembering that line in *Pilgrim's Progress* where it says that "a great darkness fell upon Christian," for the sky—although it was only mid-afternoon—was nearly black. It was obvious that a big storm was brewing up, so I turned down a track that led to a mountain lodge—a sort of rough-and-ready snowline motel—and bought myself the use of a cabin for the night. Not a moment too soon. Thunder broke roaring over the mountains, and rain fell as ferociously as if it was being forced from a fireman's hose.

My cabin was made of logs, with tiny windows that looked

out on to the enormous trunks of the fir-trees among which it was tucked. Unlike most American tourist accommodations, it had no bathroom, but—perhaps as a sort of consolation—an elderly electric stove stood on the covered porch. I made myself a meal, cleaned Daisy, spent rather longer than usual writing up my diary, and studied maps for the rest of the day.

After that, there didn't seem anything more that I actually had to do. I looked at my watch and found rather to my horror that it was still only five o'clock. I had just got to the last page of my only entertaining paperback—"last page," in this instance meaning rather more than it usually does, for so as to carry the minimum weight I had been nihilistically tearing off and throwing away each chapter as I read it—and a careful inspection of the cabin failed to reveal any left-behind books; there was no television, and to cap everything, the cabin felt cold and damp. Outside, although the thunder had died away, the rain was still falling heavily; the whole scene was about as festive as a frog's funeral, and if I was going to stay sane I was obviously going to have to take some action. I slung my anorak over my head and made a dash for the main building of the cabin complex, my rubber-soled shoes slipping on the pine needles that covered the intervening ground as if they'd been skates on ice.

The main building, which was just a larger version of my own cabin, had the air of suspended animation common to all holiday locations out of season. Its wooden tables, which in holiday months might have seemed appealingly rustic, now looked simply battered, and the hard benches beside them offered no inducement to relaxation. Even the big fireplace, which would have been so comforting had even a single log been burning in it, was dark and empty, only a few dusty piled-up fir-cones displayed on its grey ashes.

Apart from the woman who had taken my room-rent, and whom I could now glimpse clattering about in the kitchen, I was the only person in the place, so I saw that I couldn't hope for congenial company to brighten up the evening. But over in a corner I spotted a bookcase.

I peered eagerly through the locked glass doors; it held some Reader's Digest condensed books, and a few paperbacks with titles such as *Day of the Mad Dogs, Confessions of a Driving Instructor,* and *Blood and Guts is Going Nuts.* Not exactly what I would have chosen, but as an alternative to spending the next few hours just watching the rain come down the idea of getting my hands on them was sheer heaven. I tapped at the kitchen door.

"Yes?"

"I was wondering if I could borrow a book, for the evening?"

"Sorry—I haven't got none."

"One of the ones from that bookcase, perhaps? Do you have the key?"

The woman came out of the kitchen, wiping her hands on a soggy dishcloth, and trudged across the room. She was wearing a pair of those wooden-soled clogs called exercise sandals, and her footsteps sounded like the empty-coconut-shell cacophony that used, in early films, to simulate the sound of galloping hooves, but slowed down, as if the sound-track was faulty.

"Oh, them," she said enigmatically, studying the spines. I waited hopefully. "Can't let you borrow none of them," she added, with an air of finality.

"Why not? Aren't they for the guests to read?"

"Wouldn't know about that. But they're very valuable books. Couldn't let just anyone handle them."

I looked again, thinking that perhaps I had missed something. But no, they were quite definitely condensed books (three best-sellers shrunk to fit into each volume) and the equally available pulp paperbacks. But faced with the appalling idea of being left for the whole evening with nothing to read, I grew cringingly suppliant.

"I promise I'd take great care of it, if you'd let me borrow one. Just for this evening? I'd bring it back before I leave tomorrow."

But nothing would move her. Like the biblical lawyers who

took away the key of knowledge she retreated into the kitchen, leaving me glaring frustratedly at the locked glass doors.

I put a quarter into an automatic vending machine, and ate an over-sweet bar of chocolate that I didn't really want; then I studied a brochure that assured me that this particular district was not only ideal for honeymooners but also afforded matchless facilities for catching Dolly Varden trout. (A really keen man could, I suppose, scoop the jackpot by romancing a bride with the maiden name of Varden.) For a really diverting thrill, I even leant on a window-sill and watched the rain come down. Finally, though, I turned to crime.

Alone in the dimly-lit room, armed with a steak-knife purloined from a serving-table drawer, it was the work of only a moment to prise open the lock of the bookcase; then I was off across the dripping yard, my printed trophy tucked secretively under the shelter of my anorak.

Back in my cabin, I fed logs into an old oil-drum that, connected to an iron smoke-pipe, formed an amazingly efficient stove, and tucked myself happily up in the big, lumpy bed. To add to my enjoyment, the thunderstorm returned; next to riding on a bus with a can of cold beer, which I had so relished in Kansas, I couldn't at that moment imagine any greater pleasure than lying under an old eiderdown in that little log cabin, warmed right to the tips of my toes by a crazy glowing stove, and reading a really trashy paperback to the music of the thunder and rain.

Before I left, very early the next morning, I tiptoed across the yard with the book wrapped in a plastic bag, hoping to sneak it back into its glass prison before the (so to speak) wardress was around. But the door of the main cabin was still firmly locked; all I could do was to lean the book—safe inside the bag—against the frame and bicycle quickly off.

Time had changed back yet another hour. Already I had passed from the Eastern time of the Atlantic seaboard, through the Central time of the great plains, and into the Mountain time of the Rockies and beyond. Now I was in Pacific time—

three hours behind the time of the place where I had started my trip and eight hours different to the time in England. Wheeling off in that misty dawn, I had the agreeable sensation of having got up an hour earlier, without having had to make the effort of actually doing so.

It was definitely a morning that called for an early start, because ahead lay 65 miles of wilderness country. If I broke down or had an accident, there would be no friendly garage to help me with repairs, no telephone to lift to ask for aid, no house to which I could walk for help. I just had to get through the next blank bit of map entirely on my own, with whatever food I happened to have with me. And I had to do it before dark.

The sensation was a bit like the one I had just before producing my first baby—a realisation that there was absolutely no alternative but to go ahead. The only difference was that, when it came to crossing a wilderness on a bicycle, I had only got myself to blame, whereas the responsibility for the baby could be at least partly laid at the door of another party.

It was still so early that not all of the nocturnal animals had gone to bed. A long-tailed jumping mouse sprang nervously along the edge of the road, made an unsignalled right turn, and vanished among the grasses of the verge; from the shelter of an overhanging creek-bank a pointy-nosed, black-spectacled face peered out momentarily, then sharply withdrew—a raccoon, disturbed in its hunt for a snack of frog.

The road ran imperceptibly downwards, following the curves of the Lochsa river; at first, this looked no more than a rough mountain stream, but it soon widened, and before long I was bicycling alongside a turbulent rock-strewn river. On either side, forests rose steeply towards the mountains behind them. The crannies of the rocks that flanked the road were washed with brilliant drifts of wild flowers. Dog-toothed violets, purplish-brown leopard lilies, greenish-yellow fairybells and golden-yellow fritillaries, pink fairy-slipper orchids, sky-blue wild hyacinths—I would have missed almost all of them had I been travelling by car, but on my bicycle I could not only spy them, but stop, and stare, and marvel at their beauty.

As I had already discovered in Yellowstone, my bicycle didn't frighten animals, and during the day I found myself sharing the wilderness glades with deer, red squirrels, and the long-tailed weasels whose white winter fur is ermine. Far away in the forests, mountain lions yowled like love-sick tom-cats, and above a distant crag eagles, wings extended, balanced themselves on uprising currents of air.

Towards evening I reached a point where the river that I had been following was joined by another; ahead was a churning trefoil of water where the rivers united and continued their journey as one. Between the converging rivers lay a flat meadow paved with golden drifts of buttercups; it reminded me of my first Appalachian camp-ground, and once again defying the rule about not pitching a tent near running water, I camped among the flowers. Every muscle ached from the length of the day's journey. Daisy also had felt the strain; the tread on her front tyre had worn completely flat—the wheel had, I calculated, revolved nearly 94,000 times since breakfast.

By noon the next day I had—for the time being—finished bicycling west and was once more heading south, through country that reminded me again of Switzerland. Many of the small wooden houses had ancient lilac bushes in their gardens, a sign that they themselves had been there a long time, for one of the first jobs of a settler's wife had been to plant a lilac bush, to signify the metamorphosis of a mere shelter into a home. Handsome old barns sat with the established air of senior citizens in wooden-fenced upland pastures, and docile cattle nosed for water in pretty, tumbling streams. It was a peaceful, harmonious patch of country, where I would have liked to sit around and rest, but the weather had turned colder even than it had been in Butte, and I had to keep moving to stay warm.

Soon the road started to climb and it wasn't only the movement that kept me warm—it was the effort of pushing Daisy uphill. Not for the first time, I was glad that I was travelling alone, for if I had been with other bicyclists—who would certainly have had ten-speed gears—I would have been an intolerable drag. As it was, I just got off the three-speed Daisy whenever a gradient got too hard, and walked; it was, as I had already found out, a slow way of traversing a continent but it would, I still felt sure, get me across in the end.

Up, up, up went the road. Fences vanished, and the placid browsing cattle gave place to restless, tussock-snatching sheep. Soon there were no more houses and, rising abruptly above the tree-line, I had the feeling of a swimmer who, at the end of a deep dive, suddenly surfaces into the open air. All the world seemed to lie below me in a vast panorama of wind-swept mountain-tops, while above, clouds as grey as storm-lashed ocean rollers tumbled in a sky that might, for all I could see of its limits, have stretched from pole to pole.

Somewhere along this most dramatic road I crossed, in a north-to-south direction, the 45th parallel, which I had previously crossed, going from south to north, soon after I had left Yellowstone, and which I would have to cross again (south-north) if I was going to carry out my plan of bicycling up the Oregon coast.

IDAHO AND OREGON

Grangeville, outside which I camped the following night, had about it all the natural severity of upland towns; it seemed to me like a larger edition of a Scotch village named Tomintoul, which lies on a bleak highland pass and was once voted, by my husband and me, the Place We Would Least Like to Spend Our Honeymoon In. But the coffee shop in the main street turned out fantastic waffles and I left town in something of a hurry, partly because of a danger of succumbing—like King John with lampreys—to a surfeit of waffles, and partly because I was agog to reach the next marker on my map—White Bird, Idaho.

White Bird. What a romantic name. It just had to live up to it, I told myself, trying not to remember the early lesson I had learnt about American names ("if a town is called Megalopolis, that means it's only got one tap"). It was, I had read, a steep ten-mile descent with twelve hair-pin bends and would, the guide-book assured me, be a "scenic experience." For once, the guide-book was dead right.

I stood at the top of White Bird and gazed, entranced, at the view spread out in front of me. In the foreground the brown foothills dropped steeply away, streaked with the green of valleys and ric-racked by the grey ribbon of the road. Beyond the descending foothills, the land dropped out of sight, only to rise again on the far side of what must have been a distant depression; it then took off into yet more rising brown and green hills, and finished on the far horizon with range after range of blue and mauve and purple mountains. And most extraordinary of all, in this gigantic scene there was—apart from the road and a few telegraph poles—absolutely nothing that had been made by man. No houses, no factories, no chimneys, no smoke, not even —for once—the vapour-trail of a passing plane. It was hard to believe that I was in America, for—although by now I had seen quite a few of them—I still couldn't get used to the vast empty spaces that existed inside the richest country on earth.

I got out my camera, and resting it on a bollard designed to stop cars tumbling over a particularly steep drop, swung it around in a succession of overlapping shots. The resulting panorama, when developed at home, showed quite clearly something which I hadn't noticed while I was pressing the shutter; most of the scene is in bright, cloud-dappled sunshine, but from one corner, bearing down on the camera like an enormous and rather grubby lace curtain, is the outline of the mother and father of all storms.

The storm hit me just as I reached the last of the hair-pin bends, first as hail and then—less stingingly painful but more difficult to bicycle through—as snow. I battled across the foothills, down into the previously-hidden depression, and up through the second lot of foothills. By now the snow was driving almost horizontally; it caught in the trees and ravines of the mountain canyon into which the road was leading me, piling up even as I looked into great drifts and banks.

I couldn't go back, but at the same time I was scared of going forward. I got out my map, to try to see if there were any villages to the right or left of the road, but even as I unfolded it, the snow obliterated the map's small print, so that I was left holding little more than a wilting square of crystal-laden paper. Luckily, I remembered enough of the map to know that I was on quite a big road, and, feeling that my best bet was to stay on it, I ate some chocolate and—there being no way I could ride on that snowy surface—went on pushing Daisy up the hill.

I was walking with my head bent down, trying to keep my

half-frozen chin inside the collar of my anorak, and I almost hit
the timber lorry before I even realised it was there. It was one of
those enormous transporters that, extended to their full length,
carry whole trees from the forests to the sawmills and then, on
the empty return journey, hitch their rearmost wheels up on to
their centre-sections, so as to become both shorter and speedier
for the non-paying part of the round trip. A man was walking
crab-wise round the parked transporter, checking the chains that
secured his load; he was stamping his feet as he moved, so that I
momentarily had the impression that he was doing some sort of
traditional dance. He halted and smiled at me, snow clinging to
the unshaved bristles of his chin.

"Hi there! Taking a little walk?"

I couldn't think of a suitably jokey reply. "Is there any town
this way? Quite soon?"

The man looked at me quizzically. "Depends what you mean
by 'soon.' Fifteen—twenty miles, maybe. That soon enough for
you?"

I may have looked as if I was going to burst into tears. I certainly felt like it.

"Care for a ride?" suggested the man kindly.

I could only nod. Jamming Daisy between two of the tree-
trunks that formed his load, he grabbed me round my middle.

"Up you go," he cried, boosting me into the cab. Clambering
in on the other side, he swung the enormous transporter back on
the road as nonchalantly as a mother altering the position of a
pram.

Inside, the cab was as snug as Toad's gipsy caravan. Astern of
our heads, a narrow bunk spilled rumpled blankets from behind
a partly-drawn chintz curtain. Photographs of dark-haired children were pinned to the dashboard, alongside a worn St. Chris-
topher medallion, and the floor carried a drift of discarded newspapers, flattened Coke cans, and crumpled candy wrappers.
Over the pillow of the bunk I could just glimpse a small gilt
crucifix; under it, a vase shaped like an ice-cream cone held
some dried grasses and a single scarlet plastic rose.

Through the now-clear, now-flake-speckled arc of the windscreen wipers I peered out at fir trees loaded and loaded and again loaded with falling snow, at lakes furrowed and pitted with frozen spray, at lee-side crags as black as coal and weatherside rocks as white as frosted Christmas cakes. And all the time, the road went up and up. On my own, there wasn't a hope that I would have made it; I looked at the driver, and he looked at me, and over the intervening gearbox we exchanged smiles, both knowing—without words—what the other was thinking.

The transporter was very noisy and words were, in fact, more or less useless. To hear each other speak, we had to lean together until our heads were nearly touching, and soon after we had gone through the formality of exchanging names we gave up trying. Occasionally the driver, taking one hand off the wheel, would open some box or packet and offer me something to eat. We would travel along munching companionably; it was the first almost totally wordless friendship I had ever established, and after the barrage of questions that was normally fired at me the restfulness of it was agreeably relaxing.

Hours passed. We dropped down from the mountains into an open, rolling plain, over which the shadows of clouds followed each other rapidly, like travellers released from the scrutiny of a passport control. Here, no snow had fallen, and when we got out of the cab the air had about it a faint suggestion of spring.

"Got to get some gas. And mebbe some real food."

"I'd love to offer you a meal."

"Naw, naw. Let me treat you to a steak sandwich. Like steak sandwiches? That is, if you wouldn't mind."

"Mind what?"

"Eatin' with me."

"Why on earth should I? I'd be delighted—but you really must let me pick up the check."

Arguing amicably, we went into a roadside café and ordered steak sandwiches, which turned out to be minced hamburger meat lying on gravy-soaked slices of bread. Watching him wipe the last scrap of bread round in the last smear of gravy, I thought again of what the driver had said—about eating with him.

"Why did you ask if I'd 'mind' eating with you?"

He grinned, and shrugged with a sideways motion that was at once deprecating and ingratiating.

"Oh . . . I dunno. But some folks might."

I still couldn't understand. "But why?"

"On account of my being—well, dark-skinned."

I honestly hadn't noticed. "But you . . . you just look sort-of sun-tanned."

He shook his head, spearing the quarter of tomato that had decorated his sandwich and cramming it into his already-full mouth as if, by chewing, he could legitimately delay his next remark. After a moment, he placed the fork parallel to the knife, which already lay across the top of his plate, swallowed deliberately, wiped his mouth, and announced—with the cautious air of a small boy confessing to some playground crime—"I'm Mexican."

Still I waited, unaware that this fact could constitute a reason for not sharing a table. He moved a sauce-bottle across the cloth, aligned it with a salt-shaker, thought better of the project, and moved the bottle back to its original place.

"Some folks, they don't like eatin' with us Mexicans. Time was, we couldn't even go into some eatin' places. Different now, of course. But still, I wouldn't want to force myself on anyone. . . ."

I was astounded. I had heard, of course, about the attitude that some white Americans—particularly the Mormons—had towards blacks, but I had no idea that there was also prejudice against other colours of skin. Looking at the friendly brownish face on the far side of the sauce-bottle, I felt indignation rising. I wanted to ask this kind man exactly what had happened to him in the past, and to take some sort of action to see that it didn't happen again. But it was just too big a subject, and too big a problem; I could only encompass what could be achieved in the immediate present.

"There's no question of you forcing yourself on me, Mr. Gonzales. I'm extremely grateful to you for rescuing me and I'm very happy to be eating with you. Now, what'll we have for afters?"

We pushed aside our steak plates and consolidated our friendship with slices of Pie Ala (which is apple pie topped with vanilla ice cream and used to be called—when the idea first spread from the kitchens of French-speaking settlers—Pie à la Mode) and finished off the meal with malted milk sodas.

Perhaps I was unconsciously trying, by overeating, to convince Mr. Gonzales that I was sincerely glad to be sharing a meal with him. The only immediate effect was, however, that as soon as I got back to the cab I fell into a python-like sleep. I woke to find that we had come to a halt in the delivery yard of a sawmill.

"Hey! Wake up! This is as far as I go."

Already giant grabs were swinging out over the transporter; I leapt out, fearing to see Daisy fly up into the air. But someone had already parked her neatly by an office door.

"Which way out?" I yelled, over the general noise.

"Thatta way. But why don't you have a look around, since you're here? Tell 'em Gonzo sent you."

I pushed open the door of the office and went in. A large, cheerful looking man in shirt sleeves was talking on the telephone.

"So I says to her, 'If your husband's as hard a worker as you're pretty-looking, I'll give him a job any day of the week.'"

He noticed me, and put his hand over the mouthpiece. "Hello there—you wanting a job?"

"Not really. I was just wondering if I could have a look round. Mr. Gonzales suggested I ask."

"Gonzo? What's he think we're running here—Disneyland?" He took his hand from the mouthpiece. "I'll call you back, feller."

"Please—I don't want to be a nuisance. It's just that I've never seen an American sawmill. . . ."

He swung his chair round to face me. "Got a fifty-dollar tour just starting. That suit you?"

My face must have fallen like Newton's apple. He laughed delightedly.

"Hell, I was just teasin'. Have a cup of coffee, then I'll show you round myself. Slack around the office today. Be glad to."

In the first shed a tree-trunk the size of a space-missile was thundering down a steel-floored chute. Nearby, in a glass-sided, metal-banded den not unlike a telephone-booth, a man sat in a state of obviously intent concentration.

The noise was deafening. "Highest-paid man in the plant," shouted my guide. "Squares up the logs—decides which shape a log'll cut up into best. Has to make up his mind in a coupla seconds—decisions that'll fix the profits of the whole darn outfit. Very skilled operator."

In front of the man was a sloping control panel hardly larger than a typewriter. He pressed a button, and instantly giant circular saws ripped off two sides of the tree-trunk. Another button, and spikes like the teeth of a gargantuan crocodile shot out from the sides of the chute and jabbed at the trunk, rotating it as if it had been weightless; with a noise like jet engines thrown suddenly into reverse the saws bit a second time into the wood, trimming it into the shape of a flat-sided railway-carriage.

A final stab of a finger on a button, and steel rollers—as large as the human bodies on which the Juggernaut idols were once propelled—trundled the log out of sight. Immediately another untrimmed log crashed into position alongside the saws.

In the enormous mill I lost track of the number of operations done on the wood; we walked through one cavernous building after another, while mind-numbingly noisy machines attacked the timber, ripping and shaping and planing it with relentless efficiency and speed.

Towards the end of the production line, we went into a shed where a row of women stood watching a moving belt. It carried shortish lengths of wood; as they spotted a length that had a knot in it they picked it off the belt, ripped out the knotted section on small individual circular saws, and replaced the now knot-free timber on the moving belt. Behind each woman stood a container, into which she threw the knotted portions.

"Make chipboard out of them," said my guide. "Never so much as a single knot in any timber that goes out of here," he added proudly.

In an adjoining shed, more women supervised machines that cut dovetails on the knotless sections, spread glue on the dovetails, and rammed the sections together into flawless lengths.

"We've always got a waiting list of women, wanting to work here. We pay very good money. They're usually working for something definite—new washing-machine, colour television, something like that. Makes them really keen." In the dispatch building, the women were moving from place to place with unsmiling urgency, like commuters hurrying to catch a longed-for evening train.

As I paused to look back on the mill town from the barren hills beyond it I could see—apart from the inevitable soulless Main Street—very little except for the vast mill and a sprawling complex of caravan homes. Even though I was several miles away I could still faintly hear the noise of the machinery and the crash and thump of the rolling logs. But up there in the hills, I could also hear the skylarks.

By noon the following day I had reached Boise, Idaho. It was a large, busy town and as I bicycled through the suburbs I suddenly felt incredibly weary. Not just weary in my muscles, but bone-weary—physically and mentally completely at the end of my resources. I thought that if I had to travel another mile, or hear another car-horn, or answer another well-intentioned question, I would fall to bits.

I bought some food and, asking which was the best motel in town, pedalled towards it with all the urgency of an about-to-be father driving his wife to the maternity home.

"Do you care for blue, green or brown, ma'am?"

"What?"

The desk clerk was patient. "Blue, green or brown—our rooms

are all decorated in one of those three shades. Which colour would you prefer?"

I had visions of lagoons, of summer skies, of sapphires, of all things bright and bluetiful.

"Blue," I said unhesitatingly.

There then followed what must surely have been the least favourite twenty minutes in the life of the room clerk. He showed me the first blue room—no, it was too small. The second overlooked a car-park. In the third, I could hear the piped music from the swimming pool. The fourth didn't have a double bed— and that day, only the biggest bed in the business was going to be large enough to satisfy me. Finally he unlocked the door of a room that, he warned me, cost more than any of the others; decorated in shades of the purest blue, looking out on to a private, plant-greened patio, it had not only a bathroom fit for a *fille de joie* but also the largest, most exactly-right bed that I could possibly imagine.

Recklessly handing over a wad of dollars, I bathed with an extravagant profusion of fluffy blue towels, ate a picnic meal of cold tongue, fresh fruit and Californian Chablis, and fell blissfully into the enormous bed. Just before I closed my eyes, I glanced at my watch. It was still only three o'clock in the afternoon.

I must have slept for nearly twenty hours, for I only just checked out in time to avoid paying a second day's rent. Miraculously, I felt totally revived.

From Grangeville to Boise I had been travelling—because of the lack of east-west roads through the forests—almost due south; now, full of both energy and enthusiasm, I again started heading west. It was the last main turn of direction on my road to the Pacific and nothing, I felt, must now be allowed to stand in the way of getting there.

Then, biting on an apple, I pulled an inlay out of one of my teeth. There was that jagged lump of metal—looking like something scooped off the surface of the moon—and here was this hole in one of my teeth, feeling, under the apprehensive probing

of my tongue, about as big as the Grand Canyon. Clearly, the
two were going to have to be reunited.

Around me, at that particular moment, was a very large, very
empty bit of Oregon, USA. There wasn't a dentist, it was pretty
safe to guess, for at least 50 miles in any direction.

Carefully, I prised the moon-fragment out of the apple and
placed it in the tiny box where I kept spare tyre valves. Then,
having heard how expensive dentists were in America, I scrooge-
ily got out my medical insurance policy and studied the section
headed Dental Treatment. Hmmm . . . well, I obviously
couldn't claim under the heading of Loss Of Dentures, Other
Than By Breakage During Mastication, nor under Temporary
Total Disablement, but there didn't seem to be any reason why
this shouldn't be called an Unspecified Emergency. I bicycled
on, occasionally giving a tentative suck at the Grand Canyon.

I'm not exactly sure whether I went up very high or whether,
that day, the sky had come down very low, but what I do know
is that after a while I was groping along in the middle of one of
the coldest, wettest rainclouds that had been around since the
time of the Ark. After what felt like a hundred years of reeling
about in this newts' nirvana I finally made it over the top of the
mountains, and, exiting from the underside of the cloud, caught
a brief glimpse of a stupendous panorama of more bare mountains, this time streaked with greenish valleys which were, in
turn, dotted with brownish farms. But only moments after I had
escaped from the cloud, it changed its mind about letting me go,
and let loose a downpour of rain so vicious that it felt like hail.
Then it started to snow.

"*You can't do this to me*," I found myself yelling at the
swirling driving flakes. "I won't be stopped, I won't, *I won't*."
My despairing shout faded down the desolate road, deflected off
the telegraph poles that receded in ever-diminishing perspective,
their outlines blurred in the grey-white holocaust. Behind the
poles, morose cattle stood tail-end to the storm, their heads
drooping as if almost begging for a slaughterer's hammer. An occasional iron windmill creaked complainingly, as if to protest

that even a mechanical object should not have to stay outdoors on a day so bitter, so utterly grim.

My tooth, aggravated by the cold, was aching remorselessly. It was incredible to think that when I had passed through St. Louis there had been a heatwave, and that, looking ahead, mid-summer day lay only a few weeks in the future.

I had been right in guessing that the first dentist would be about 50 miles away, but I had to travel a further 150 to get my tooth fixed, as his receptionist said he couldn't see me for a week. Perhaps this was my own fault—I shouldn't have blurted out that I was bicycling, because, faced with a story that was, to her, so obviously untrue, she clearly didn't believe the other part of my tale—that I was in considerable pain. Being in the tetchy state of mind that people sometimes get into when suffering from the impression that someone is trying to galvanise their maxillary nerves by plugging live wires into their ears, I exited from the surgery—nobly restraining myself from slamming the door—and stormed off down the street, convinced that I would find a more sympathetic receptionist round the next corner. But of course, that had been the only dental surgery in the town.

Some days later, I coasted downhill out of the Willamette National Forest into Eugene, Oregon, a university town that I felt sure bred dentists with all the profligacy of God creating stars. Here was one, on the very first corner. His brass plate was so large that he just had to be good—either that, or he had a brother-in-law in the brass engraving business. I rang the bell. How lucky you are, said a curvy white-uniformed receptionist—the doctor just happens to have a cancellation. Wait here, please.

I sat down, studied some magazines with names like *Cosmopolitan* and *Glamour*, and waited for the attention of the doctor. A door opened.

"Come in, please."

I sat down in the chair, which immediately tilted over backwards, so that I was lying as prone as a pancake.

"I've dropped this inlay out of my tooth. . . ."

"Splendid. Splendid." His voice held the same soothing reassurance as those aircraft announcements that lull you into believing that the wings aren't really going to fall off—they're *meant* to flex up and down in that scarey way.

"Perhaps you'd care to tell me a little about yourself? Have you ever had a serious accident involving head injuries?"

"Oh no—this wasn't a serious accident. I was just eating an apple."

"Do you have night sweats accompanied by weight loss or cough?"

"Really, it's hardly affected me at all. Apart from hurting, that is."

"Do you have pain in or near your ears?"

"No, it's just in my tooth; that's what I've really come about —this tooth. The one with the hole."

"Indeed yes. Of course. Tell me, now, has any physician ever informed you that you have a tumor or growth?"

What was this, a major surgery unit? I lifted my head from the tissue-covered pillow and, squinting round, saw that the doctor was not, as I'd innocently supposed, getting ready to look into my mouth, but was sitting at a desk, ticking off squares on a list headed Patient Medical History.

"Please, do we have to go through all these questions? All I really need is to have the inlay cemented back. I've got it, here."

With the sigh of a man resigned, against his better judgment, to humouring an uneducated and probably also rather backward vole, the doctor got up and placed himself in the On Your Marks position, behind my head.

"Would you care to let me see it?"

Gingerly, I opened my little box, but what fell out on to the doctor's meticulously-scrubbed hand was not a precious-metal inlay (which was later found crouching at the bottom of the box) but three grubby rubber tyre valves. While I was paying my bill, I took a peek at that Patient Medical History list, and the next question was going to have been Are You Pregnant? Perhaps, on the whole, I got off rather lightly.

When I finally left Eugene, it was as if on wings. It was a beautiful sunny morning, my toothache had gone, and—most wonderful of all—I was at last within striking distance of the Pacific. Only one stretch of open country, one range of mountains, and one forest now lay between me and the ocean. It wasn't much over 50 miles, and I was determined to do it in a day.

Like the final act in a Christmas pantomime, America pulled out all the stops to make the last stage beautiful. Up, up I went into a tree-lined pass, great avenues of conifers framing views of rolling hills. Lakes as bright as newly-minted coins flickered in the valleys, and everywhere the air was filled with the songs of birds. Then, as I started the final descent to the Pacific, the flowers began. Rhododendron, lilac and peach-blossom breasted the garden fences with all the lavishness of a Japanese flower festival, cyclamen peeked from the sheltering overhang of weeping birches. Every flower of an English spring garden seemed to be in bloom, tucked into informal beds or scattered like confetti in the woodland glades. As I passed small village sawmills, even the cut wood seemed to smell not of resin but of orange-blossom.

American road-signs don't often record distances and, lacking a milometer, I had no way of telling exactly how near I was getting to the coast. Each time the road went downwards I hoped that at last I was going to see the ocean, but again and again the road went down only to go up again. I passed pretty lakes, edged with holiday houses—each with its own landing-stage—and country cottages with riding horses feeding peacefully in wood-fenced paddocks. Hamlets came and went, with churches and playing-fields and homely grocery stores; they all looked delightful places in which to linger, but I didn't halt, for by now I felt an obsessive need to reach the coast.

At last, as night was falling, I wheeled into Florence, the town which, on my map, had been marked as actually being on the ocean. But to my chagrin, the map hadn't been entirely accurate; the ocean was there, yes, but between it and the town lay

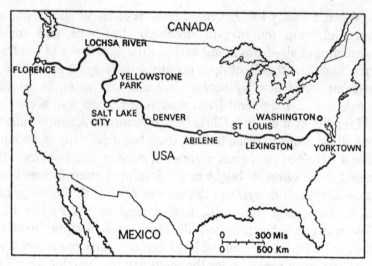

FLORENCE, OREGON

a big stretch of sand-dunes. There was no possible way I could cross these in the dark. At the very last moment, the Pacific had eluded me. All I could do was pitch my tent and wait for morning.

OREGON, AND HOME AGAIN

The emotion that I experienced when finally I reached the Pacific made me feel quite like Cortes, who, standing "silent, upon a peak in Darien" had—according to Keats—stared at it "with a wild surmise." I had been listening to it, with mounting excitement, for quite a time before it actually came into view. It made a muffled roaring sound, like the engines of jet planes warming up on a distant runway. Then, rounding a corner, I at last saw it—the ocean towards which I had been bicycling for all those arduous weeks.

Only a scatter of dunes separated me from an immense beach, on to which mile-long breakers were tumbling with relentless force; it was a stupendous sight—the sea and sky a brilliant blue against the white of the breakers and the gold of the sand. And —an unexpected delight—the dunes were splashed with vivid pools of yellow and orange flowers; along the edge of the road, great swathes of mauve lupins tossed their pagoda-heads in the fresh in-shore breeze, while behind me, on the landward side, banks of canary-coloured broom cascaded prodigally down from wind-bent, stunted woods.

I bicycled northwards, the road hugging the ocean, every bend revealing fresh panoramas of enormous empty beaches and more apparently endless miles of thundering breakers. Where the sand gave way to rocks, great herds of sealions chattered and

squabbled above the water-line, the dark pelts of the adults contrasting with the browny-gold fur of their pups.

Cape Perpetua loomed ahead—a vast 40 million-year-old ba-
salt headland, sighted by Captain Cook in 1778 and named by
him for Saint Perpetua, martyred in Carthage some 200 years
after the birth of Christ. Short of swimming, there was no way
round this immense barrier, so I just had to walk up it, pushing
Daisy, and it was evening when I coasted down the other side
into a pleasant little seaside town.

Smelt fishers were out along the shore, wading into the surf
with their big triangular-framed nets; among the rocks of the
foreshore families were fanning driftwood fires, ready for grilling
the catch. It was clearly an evening for celebration, so I bought
some wine and invited the fishermen to join me. Yes please,
they said, but may we make it a little later, when we've stopped
fishing—and you will join us for supper, won't you?

I sat on the low cliffs, watching them; from below came the
scent of glowing driftwood, while in front of me, spattered with
the silhouettes of sooty shearwater gulls, lay the immensity of
the Pacific Ocean, orange-gold in the horizontal rays of the setting sun.

There's nothing out there, I told myself, gazing at the gilded,
limitless horizon—nothing but waves and water, all the way to
Hawaii; I can't bicycle any more, I don't need to, I've got to the
end of the road. And I hugged Daisy; I felt sure that, if she
could have, she'd have hugged me back.

About a week later, having bicycled up the wild, beautiful Oregon coast, I caught a plane back to England; just before it
climbed to the stratospheric heights of inter-continental flight, I
caught a last glimpse of America, lying far below, partly ob-
scured by cumulonimbus clouds. A pin-prick of light flashed
briefly up, reflected perhaps from the windscreen of a car, reminding me that there were people down there.

But I hardly needed this reminder; the country over which I
would now be carried so impersonally was no longer alien to me.
On a narrow line—in some places only a few yards wide—drawn

across the United States, I felt I knew each rise and fall in the road, each bird, each tree, each flower. America would never again, to me, be just a map—it would be a living world.

I reached home on a summer evening. All the familiar English birds were singing in my garden and my eldest grandson, I was happy to hear, was expected back at any moment from a game of cricket. He came crashing in, in the usual fashion of boys, which means, of course, that he opened the door but didn't shut it again, threw sports gear on to a velvet-covered sofa, and gave the cat such a fright that she had to take refuge on the mantelpiece.

"Oh hello, Granny. You're back. That's nice." And he came over and gave me a big hug. But then I saw his eyes wander over my shoulder, in the direction of the kitchen.

"What's for supper?" he asked hopefully.

I was—quite definitely—home.